Cont

About the Author

John Parr is a Church of England priest in Suffolk. Since his ordination in 1979 he has also served in parishes in the dioceses of Liverpool and Ely. He has been involved in the training of lay people and ordained ministers in Cambridge and East Anglia, and has also worked in mental health advocacy in Suffolk. For 10 years he was a commissioning editor for Bible Reading Fellowship's *Guidelines* notes, and currently writes for *Roots* lectionary-based resources. He and his wife Frances have five grown-up children and three grandchildren.

CREDIBLE
WITNESSES

What people thought of Jesus as revealed in John's Gospel

JOHN
PARR

kevin
mayhew

kevin
mayhew

First published in Great Britain in 2016 by Kevin Mayhew Ltd
Buxhall, Stowmarket, Suffolk IP14 3BW
Tel: +44 (0) 1449 737978 Fax: +44 (0) 1449 737834
E-mail: info@kevinmayhew.com

www.kevinmayhew.com

9 8 7 6 5 4 3 2 1 0

ISBN 978 1 84867 875 0
Catalogue No. 1501539

Cover design by Rob Mortonson
© Image used under licence from Shutterstock Inc.
Edited by Virginia Rounding
Typeset by Angela Selfe

Printed and bound in Great Britain

Introduction
What kind of Gospel is John?

Accessible yet intriguing

The Gospel of John is in many ways the most accessible and immediate of the four we have. Its Jesus engages in conversation with a wide range of people, and uses everyday images like light, darkness, birth, death, water, wine, bread and shepherding to convey his message. John has been widely used in evangelism to introduce people to Christianity, and John 3:16 is probably the best-known and most inclusive verse in the Bible: 'For God so loved the world that he gave his only Son, so that everyone who believes in him may not perish but may have eternal life.'[1] But the Gospel is also enigmatic and mysterious, raising at least as many questions as it answers. What does it mean to be born from above, to live forever by eating and drinking the flesh and blood of Jesus, to see at the same time as being blind? In this Gospel Jesus is so humble and hospitable that he washes his disciples' feet before the last Passover-tide meal he eats with them. But in some of his sayings he seems to be less self-effacing: 'I am the bread of life, the light of the world, the good shepherd, the resurrection and the life, the way, the truth and the life, the true vine.' He speaks as if he is equal to God, one with him, the unique and exclusive way of relating to the divine reality he dares to call his 'Father'. What are we to make of this Gospel and its central figure?

The mystery deepens when we compare it with the other three (called the 'synoptic' Gospels, because their similarities allow them to be 'seen alongside' each other). John re-orders their sequence of events. He brings the cleansing of the temple from the end to the beginning (2:13-22). He has Jesus speaking what sound like eucharistic words in Galilee after the feeding of the five thousand, barely a third of the way into the narrative (6:35-59). He has Jesus travel backwards and forwards between Galilee and Jerusalem, like a traditional Jewish pilgrim visiting the holy city for the annual festivals. This enables him to spread Jesus' conflict with the Jerusalem authorities over the whole of his ministry, rather than compress it into the synoptics' final days. He devotes half of his Gospel to the last week of Jesus' life, slowing down the action to focus on the meaning of the most important events in the story of Jesus. What is happening in John's narrative?

---

1. In the preface of his commentary on John, Barnabas Lindars tells how he first became interested in it as a member of a Franciscan mission team to hop-pickers in Kent during the 1950s. Conducting a daily Bible study for the team members led him to believe that 'the Fourth Gospel is pre-eminently an evangelistic work'. See his *The Gospel of John*, London: Oliphants, 1972, p. 7.

John leaves out some of the other Gospels' highlights, and replaces them with material unique to his story. There are no accounts of Jesus' birth such as we find in Matthew and Luke; no parables with memorable and challenging characters; no healings of people said to be possessed by evil spirits. There is no institution of the Lord's Supper at his last meal with his disciples; no agony in the garden of Gethsemane before Jesus' arrest; no darkened sky when he dies, and no harrowing words of desolation at the end. Instead of the birth stories, the Gospel opens with a poetic meditation on Jesus' heavenly origin. In place of the parables we hear long and sometimes complex discourses, studded with Jesus' seven 'I am' sayings. Throughout the Gospel Jesus says less about the kingdom of God (the focus of his teaching in the other Gospels) and more about himself: where he and his authority come from and where his death will take him, though no one seems to understand either his origin or his destiny. Jesus' brief and memorable words over the bread and cup at the final Passover meal are replaced by an acted parable of washing feet, and extended meditations on the significance of his departure. Why does John tell the story of Jesus so differently?

Theological and spiritual

John and the synoptics have a lot in common, as we shall see. But there can be no doubting John's distinctiveness. This is easily misunderstood if his Gospel is seen primarily as a doctrine-oriented writing, or as Clement of Alexandria (AD 150-215) described it, a spiritual Gospel more concerned with nourishing faith than providing the 'bodily facts' of Jesus' life and ministry. There is no need to choose between these two perspectives, because John is both theological and spiritual. For most of its life his Gospel has been quarried for the building blocks of traditional Christian beliefs in the divinity and humanity of Jesus and the Trinity. These doctrines only began to be constructed at least a century after the Gospel was written, in an environment that owed more to Greek than to Jewish thinking. Today, however, many see John paying his theological dues to Jewish rather than to Greek thought.

This is not surprising, because John's Jesus is himself a Galilean Jew and regularly visits the Jewish festivals in Jerusalem as a pilgrim. He teaches in the synagogue and the public spaces of Jerusalem as a rabbi who is rooted in the Jewish scriptures. John's theological understanding of Jesus relies heavily on Jewish Wisdom writings such as Proverbs, the Wisdom of Solomon and Ecclesiasticus. Wisdom is international and universal, the enlightened search for understanding that enables people of faith to know how God has ordered the world so that they can live accordingly. Jewish Wisdom writings are full of practical advice based on careful observation. But they also have a more speculative side that sees the origins of Wisdom in heaven, with

God. Here God's wisdom is personified as a woman, Sophia in the Greek Bible. The writers of the Wisdom of Solomon and Ecclesiasticus re-tell the story of the Bible by presenting Sophia as a heavenly figure who acts as God's agent in creation, the history of God's chosen people Israel and the final judgement. John is inspired by these writers: what they say of Sophia, he says of Jesus.[2] Like Jesus, his Gospel is thoroughly Jewish yet at the same time open and accessible to the wider world.

John's openness may be one reason why his Gospel has played such a significant role in evangelism. Yet we cannot be certain that it was written as an evangelistic tract. John sets out his reason for writing at 20:31, but there is some ambiguity in our English translations. He says that he has selected from the available material on Jesus 'so that you may come to believe that Jesus is the Messiah, the Son of God, and that through believing you may have life in his name'. This is how the New Revised Standard Version (NRSV) translates the verse, and on the face of it, John writes as an evangelist. But the NRSV's footnotes offer an alternative translation, based on a difference of one letter in the Greek word for 'believe' in some ancient manuscripts. This allows us to see John writing 'so that you may continue to believe that Jesus is the Messiah, the Son of God . . .'. Was John's purpose, then, to convert unbelievers or to confirm those who already believe? Opinion is divided, and it is not possible to decide solely on the basis of the manuscript evidence.

The content of the Gospel provides the best clues to its original purpose. Many of its stories, as we shall see, are of people who come to faith in Jesus. But some of its leading characters, particularly those who are named, already have faith. John does not go to the trouble of engaging with the beliefs and aspirations of outsiders in the way that Paul does in his speech to Greek philosophers in Acts 17. Neither does he explain his basic outlook and assumptions for the benefit of those who do not share them. He seems much more concerned to strengthen hard-pressed Christians who are experiencing opposition on account of their loyalty to Jesus, or to appeal to groups from the wider Jewish family who already know about Jesus. On balance it appears that, as a spiritual Gospel, John sets out to nourish the faith of those who are already believers and appeal to others on the fringes of their communities, by using the stories of his witnesses to explore some of the key elements in the development of faith in Jesus, particularly faith that is tested. This is not to say that his Gospel should not be used in evangelism, only that it was probably not written for this purpose.

---

2. Like his contemporary, the Jewish writer Philo, John speaks of the heavenly Word rather than Wisdom. Gender is undoubtedly a factor. The Greek *sophia* is a feminine noun, whereas *logos* is masculine. Philo acts as a linguistic bridge between the Jewish Wisdom writings and John. What the Wisdom writers say of Sophia, Philo says of Logos and John says of Jesus. Selections from Jewish Wisdom writings are included in the Appendix.

Anonymous, undated and unaddressed

What do we know about the author of the Gospel, when and where it was written, and its first audience?[3] According to tradition, it was written by John the Apostle in Ephesus towards the end of the first century, but the Gospel itself offers only a few clues. Like the other Gospels, it is anonymous and says nothing about its date and place of writing. What we now call the Gospel of John is a composite work. Chapter 21 looks like a later addition, following what appears to have been the original ending in 20:30-31. The story of Jesus' meeting with the woman taken in adultery in 7:53–8:11 is missing from the oldest Gospel manuscripts, and found at various places in the wider gospel tradition, as the footnotes in Bibles indicate. But ignorance in these matters does not diminish the Gospel's worth. In 19:35, the evangelist mentions that he has access to eyewitness evidence. In 21:24, there is a reference to a trustworthy written source from someone other than himself. This Gospel, like the synoptics, comes from a culture that depends more on memory than on writing to transmit ideas. Its reliance on a combination of oral and written traditions preserved by those whom Jesus calls friends in 15:15[4] adds weight to the author's conviction that his Gospel not only depends on trustworthy testimony, but can itself be trusted.

Some recent scholarship has felt more confident about being able to read the Gospel as the story of John's community rather than of Jesus, but again this calls for caution. There are clear signs that John's audience is struggling in its relationships with the synagogue.[5] But the Gospel is also interested in appealing to groups on the fringes of its community: followers of John the Baptist, members of the synagogue who are drawn to Jesus but keep a low profile, and Samaritans.[6] In the Epistles of John, there is evidence of a rift between members of the community and a group who leave because of their beliefs.[7] Perhaps then we should speak of the Gospel's audiences, rather than of a single audience. According to the evangelist, what they have in common is that they, like Jesus, belong to the wider family of Israel. For reasons we can only guess, their relationships have become strained, and in some cases quite hostile. Jesus' discourse on the Good Shepherd may imply that one of the Gospel's aims is to draw these scattered communities together into 'one flock' around Jesus, the 'one shepherd'.

---

3. I refer throughout to the Gospel's audience rather than its readership, because the early Christian writings would originally have been heard in their communities rather than read by individuals. And for the sake of convenience, I call the author 'John' without making any assumptions about his or her identity.
4. Jesus calls his disciples 'friends' rather than 'slaves' here because he is prepared to trust them with the revelation he has received. John 15:27 suggests that John's account of Jesus is trustworthy because it is rooted in faithful testimony to Jesus 'from the beginning'. The statement in 21:24 that 'we know that his testimony is true' suggests that John's sources have been tested by others. These themes of faithful testimony, testing and trustworthiness are also found in the Letters of John (see 1 John 1:1-5; 4:1-6), which have much in common with this Gospel.
5. John 9:22, 34; 12:42; 16:1-3.
6. This is discussed further in the material on John the Baptist, Nicodemus, the Samaritan woman and Philip.
7. See 1 John 2:18-26.

Four striking features

Jesus' divine authority

John has a characteristic way of highlighting Jesus' divine authority. I have already mentioned his use of Jewish Wisdom traditions to draw out the particular and universal strands in the story of Jesus. But these writings have another equally important use. The way they imagine a divine attribute – God's wisdom – as a heavenly being sent by God into the world before returning to her heavenly home provides John with his basic theological framework. In the synoptics Jesus speaks of being 'sent' by God in his mission 'to the lost sheep of the house of Israel' (Matthew 15:24), or 'to seek out and to save the lost' (Luke 19:10). John uses Wisdom writings to fill out the meaning of this divine sending. As the embodiment of God's Sophia, Jesus is sent from heaven into the world, where he reveals what he knows of God before being rejected and returning to his heavenly home through his passion and resurrection.[8] Like Sophia, Jesus is God's light and glory, offers abundant life, calls people to become his disciples, and invites them to drink from him and feed on him.[9] Some of the most explicit Wisdom connections occur in Jesus' 'I am' sayings, which are also unique to John's Gospel, though like Jesus' talk of being sent, they also have their roots in sayings preserved in the other Gospels.[10] Jesus is therefore the living link between heaven and earth, the divine and human worlds, and can speak and act with the authority of the one he calls Father. By presenting Jesus as God's emissary and Sophia's embodiment, John has Jesus using the most exalted language to speak of his divine authority. Little wonder that his audiences throughout the Gospel narrative are intrigued, and at times deeply offended, at what he says.

Jesus and 'the Jews'

It is not difficult to come away from reading some parts of John's Gospel feeling very uneasy about the way the Jews are portrayed. Some of the language is offensive and dangerous. It would be anachronistic to describe John as anti-Jewish, but his Gospel's branding of the Jews as children of the devil in 8:44 has contributed to centuries of prejudice and violence. Some recent writers try to mitigate the worst effects of this by translating *hoi Ioudaioi* as 'the Judeans' rather than 'the Jews'. They point out that in this Gospel, *Ioudaioi* are from the territory of Judea in the way that Samaritans are from Samaria and Galileans are from Galilee.

---

8. John 1:1-2, 9-11, 14; 3:13; 6:33; 62; 16:28; 20:17.
9. John 1:4, 5, 39; 4:10-14; 5:40; 6:22-59; 7:37-39; 8:12; 10:10; 11:25.
10. 'I am' translates the Greek *ego eimi*, which in the Greek Bible renders the divine name 'I am who I am' in Exodus 3:14. The language of the 'I am' sayings owes much to the Wisdom traditions, as we shall see. Sometimes Jesus' 'I am' is no more than self-identification, though a greater authority comes to the fore in situations of conflict with the Jewish authorities (see 8:58; 18:5-6).

And *Ioudaioi* are certainly not the direct ancestors of today's Jewish people, whose origins lie much later than Jesus.[11] However, the Gospel defies such neat categorisation: those who oppose Jesus in the Galilean synagogue in Capernaum in 6:41 are also called *Ioudaioi*, and appear to be locals rather than visitors from the south. To complicate matters further, John tends to lump Jews and Pharisees together as opponents of Jesus, with little of the sensitivity towards the range of Pharisaic opinion and practice that we find in Jewish sources, and elsewhere in the Gospels for that matter. But again, we must be careful. Nicodemus is a Pharisee, and he shows some sympathy towards Jesus, though this falls short of outright support. Other Pharisees too are less hostile towards Jesus.[12]

Few would disagree that the language that John uses for the Jewish opponents of Jesus falls short of the sensitivity required after the horrors of the twentieth century. But what today's readers may regard as carelessness or stereotyping on the part of the evangelist is worth looking at more carefully. John uses *Ioudaioi* to refer to members of the family of Israel who engage with Jesus particularly, but not exclusively, in Jerusalem. Some of them are so incensed by his teaching that they persecute him and try to kill him, while others are puzzled by what he says and divided in their opinion of him. Some pass on information to the chief priests and Pharisees who govern Jerusalem, and occasionally some try to arrest him.[13]

The fact that *Ioudaioi*, Pharisees and chief priests are all involved in the plot to have Jesus arrested and executed makes it easier for John's readers to ignore the distinctions between these groups, and assume that Jesus is rejected by the Jews as a whole. The way John writes certainly makes this possible, and has allowed successive generations to read and hear him with a less than positive approach to the Jews. But there are other ways of reading Jesus' disputes with Jews. With what we now know of the diversity and competing claims to authority in the Jewish world at the time of Jesus, these disputes can be seen as examples of internal conflict, the family feuds over authority that characterised relationships between Jewish groups at the time. The Jesus movement, with its origins in the synagogue and temple, was one faction among many clamouring for recognition. The New Testament writings can be seen as a series of snapshots in the Jewish family album. Church and synagogue went their separate ways much later than the time of Jesus, and the partings of the ways took time.[14] This broad understanding of the setting of John's Gospel makes it more difficult to condemn it for being anti-Jewish, though its polemical edge may still be too sharp for a world which is understandably disturbed by passionate religious disputes.

11. This is the approach taken by Bruce J. Malina and Richard L. Rohrbaugh in their *Social Science Commentary on the Gospel of John*, Minneapolis: Fortress Press, 1998, pp. 44-46.
12. John 3:2; 7:50-52; 9:16; 19:38-42.
13. John 5:16-18; 6:41-59; 7:1, 11-13, 30, 32, 40-42, 45; 8:59; 9:16; 10:31, 39; 11:46; 12:42, 43.
14. See James D. G. Dunn, *The Partings of the Ways Between Christianity and Judaism and their Significance for the Character of Christianity*, London: SCM Press, 2006 (2nd edition).

John's polarised world

John's narrative is full of polar opposites – light and darkness, above and below, flesh and spirit, life and death, love and hate, sight and blindness, truth and lies, freedom and slavery, being of the world and not of the world. These dualisms are not simply abstract terms or symbols, but indications of the attitudes and actions of people around Jesus. If Jesus is associated with light and life, those who struggle or refuse to believe in him must belong to the darkness. If those who believe in Jesus are born of God, from above or of the Spirit, then those who do not know or accept him are born merely of blood or the will of the flesh or of man, or of the devil. If belief is associated with sight, then unbelief is a form of blindness. If Jesus has come from the heavenly realm above as the embodiment of God's love for the world, only to ascend to the Father's house through his death to prepare a place for his friends, his enemies can only belong to the world below that hates him. They neither know where he is from nor can they go there. If Jesus is the revelation of God's truth because he is sent by God who is true, his enemies must be children of the devil, the father of lies and a murderer whose essential character they display in their repeated attempts to assassinate him. As the Lamb of God who takes away the sin of the world, Jesus brings liberation from unbelief and sin, while his enemies remain in a slavery they refuse to recognise. They are trapped in a world of sin and death and judgement, from which only the Son can free them.

John's dualistic language has been described as 'anti-language' that polarises the world by creating two sharply divided realities.[15] It is not unique. It is found in Paul's letters and the Dead Sea Scrolls.[16] Those who feel at home in the world may find this way of speaking unwelcome. It appears to equate devotion to God with turning aside from the good things of creation. And it seems to suggest that we can make clear divisions between good and evil, right and wrong, when experience teaches us that life is too complicated for such over-simplifications. But there is another way of interpreting dualistic language. It is associated with a profound sense of unease. When we are anxious, we are more likely to see the world in black-and-white, either/or categories. We tend to interpret others as either being for us or against us, and make no allowance for honest questioning of our motives or actions by what in some circles is called critical friendship. When anxiety persists,

---

15. See Bruce J. Malina and Richard L. Rohrbaugh, *Social Science Commentary on the Gospel of John*, pp. 7ff, who reflect the assumption that language does not merely describe the world but creates it.

16. Galatians 5:16-26 sees the world divided into those who are driven by the desires of the flesh and those who display the fruit of the Spirit; and Romans 3–8 contrasts a world held by the powers of sin, law, flesh and death with the new world of righteousness, freedom, Spirit and life. The Community Rule from the Dead Sea Scrolls sees the world governed by the spirits of truth and falsehood, light and darkness. See Geza Vermes, *The Complete Dead Sea Scrolls in English*, London: Penguin Books, 1998, pp. 97-117. Vermes' comment on the Essenes' concentration on the blessedness of the chosen rather than the fate of the damned (p. 74) could also apply to John's Gospel, which focuses primarily on all that is associated with the positive pole.

it can seem as if the whole world is intent on undermining us. Life can feel unremittingly grim, with no signs of encouragement or hope. The roots of this way of speaking and thinking lie in the so-called 'fight or flight' response to danger. Faced by an overwhelming threat, the brain is programmed to rescue us, not by encouraging us to analyse the situation or weigh up a range of possibilities, but to overcome the threat or escape from it. On this understanding, we should not be surprised to find individuals or communities whose world feels more menacing than benevolent using dualistic language.

Among John's audiences are people whose loyalty to Jesus sets them at odds with other members of the fragmented family of Abraham and Moses. We can imagine their sense of the absence of Jesus generating feelings of abandonment that could only exacerbate the anxiety generated by local hostility. Yet if John's dualistic language speaks to their situation, it does not simply reflect or reinforce their fears. His Gospel holds out the possibility of a more creative and hopeful relationship with their anxiety and its source. Jesus has not abandoned them, but remains as a powerful presence in the sending of the Holy Spirit as God's advocate and guide. His physical absence is the consequence of his return to the heavenly realm, which he opens up as a home for them too. His departure from the world of sensory experience through the horrors of crucifixion is a glorified offering of his life that is nothing less than a prayer for the protection and wellbeing of all who believe in him, as they do.[17] They may have been disowned by institutions like the synagogue that have provided them with spiritual and cultural roots, but they now live in an alternative world that provides them with meaning and resilience. Jesus is now their temple and true vine. He is the promised prophet like Moses, who feeds them with the bread of heaven and the living water of the Spirit, the good shepherd who searches out and rescues God's flock, the hope of resurrection and eternal life, the true and living way to salvation and the true Passover lamb. John's anti-language assures them that in Jesus they find more than they have lost from the world, because in him alone all the ancient symbols of Israel reach their true fulfilment.

John's Gospel has often been interpreted as advocating a sectarian vision of life in a hostile world, with an exclusive understanding of faith and truth and God. But there are other possibilities too. The world may be hostile to Jesus and his followers, but it is still the object of God's love. Jesus may draw his disciples to himself in a secure community bound together by servant-like love, but he refuses to allow them to turn in on themselves. They are hated, not simply because they are present in the world, but because they represent their Lord, who gave himself generously and lovingly for the salvation of a world whose most

---

17. John 14:1-31; 17:1-25.

powerful forces were intent on destroying him.[18] On this understanding of John's Gospel, its anti-language is not simply a response to anxiety but a way of maintaining Jesus' own witness to life, truth and justice in the face of death-dealing, lies and oppression. There is no doubt that John's vision of God is sharply focused in Jesus, but it can hardly be narrow and exclusive when he is intent on reaching out to the 'other sheep' of the wider family of Israel and beyond.[19] If the beleaguered communities to whom the Gospel is addressed are to 'love one another as I have loved you', their calling takes them beyond themselves to embrace the world of flesh and blood in which their heavenly Lord was God's Sophia-Logos incarnate.

A long line of witnesses

Mention of witness brings out a fourth distinctive feature of John's Gospel. The Gospel's Prologue interweaves the Wisdom poetry of Sophia-Logos with lines about the witness of John the Baptist in 1:7-8 and 19. The Baptist's mission is continued by many of the Gospel's characters, beginning with the first followers of Jesus in Judea and culminating in the witness of the anonymous and enigmatic 'disciple whom Jesus loved', whose writings are acknowledged as 'true testimony' in 21:24. Sometimes in this Gospel, witness to Jesus is clear and unambiguous: John the Baptiser's 'Here is the Lamb of God, who takes away the sin of the world!' (1:29); Andrew's 'We have found the Messiah' (1:41); the Samaritan woman's 'Come and see a man who told me everything I have ever done! He cannot be the Messiah, can he?' (4:29); Simon Peter's 'Lord, to whom can we go? You have the words of eternal life' (6:68); the formerly blind man's 'Lord, I believe' in 9:38; Martha's 'Yes, Lord, I believe that you are the Messiah, the Son of God, the one coming into the world' (11:27); Mary Magdalene's 'I have seen the Lord' (20:18); Thomas' 'My Lord and my God!' (20:28). Confessions like these seem to fly in the face of what we read in the other Gospels about the disciples' hesitations and uncertainties over Jesus. John certainly compresses the development of faith in Jesus by presenting hard-won belief as fully formed at the outset. But at the same time, as we shall see, he outlines the way that faith develops. It does not simply arrive as a package to be unwrapped.

John's Gospel never loses sight of the role of ambiguity, mystery and non-knowing in faith. John includes the testimony of half-belief and unbelief, alongside the probing and questioning that are proper to mature and maturing faith. Thomas is the archetypal sceptic, who finds his way to faith by refusing to believe. Philip too is not easily convinced when Jesus speaks of knowing the Father through him. Who knows what to make of the secret witness of Nicodemus and Joseph of Arimathea?

---

18. John 3:16; 13:34, 35; 14:15-24; 15:16-27; 17:14-19; 20:21.
19. John 10:16; 12:32.

For some of his followers, Jesus is more mystery than they can manage. Some find his teaching about the bread of life too difficult, and in 6:66 they withdraw from his company. Like his brothers in 7:5, they seem not to believe in him, though their unbelief does not turn into outright rejection and violence.

Speaking of Jesus

John includes a wide spectrum of witnesses to Jesus. Though he would find some of them more commendable than others, I hope he would agree that they all convey a credibility that reflects their place in his account. Their responses to Jesus invite those who hear and read this Gospel to identify with them in whatever ways they can. In this book I follow John's lead by allowing many of his characters to speak about Jesus by telling their stories. This involves imagination and a degree of fiction at times. In each of the chapters of this book, a character's testimony is illuminated with some background information, before going on to show how John uses the testimony as part of the witness of his Gospel as a whole. Each chapter ends with some reflections that help to draw John's Gospel into the present. By writing about John's Gospel like this, I hope that its witness will enter our own imagination and experience, and find new audiences who will become part of that long line of witnesses stretching back to the Judean desert and the words of another John.

ONE

John the Evangelist

John 1:1-18

Background

Each of the four Gospels begins differently. Matthew starts with a genealogy that traces Jesus' line back to Abraham, to introduce his account of Jesus' conception, birth and childhood. Mark begins in the wilderness with John the Baptist, who baptises Jesus in the Jordan and prepares him to embark on his ministry. Luke weaves together the accounts of two unexpected pregnancies and subsequent births, to the elderly Elizabeth and the young woman Mary. John's beginning goes back much further. The words and themes of his Prologue in 1:1-18 echo the creation story that opens the Jewish scriptures.

Scholars of an earlier generation saw John speaking the language of Greek philosophy with his talk of 'the Word' (logos in Greek), perhaps in an attempt to relate the gospel of Jesus the Jew to the ideas of the culture that dominated his world. Though logos certainly allows John to speak into the wider Greek world, where logos is the universal reason or mind, his Gospel is now more often seen as a fundamentally Jewish work. Jewish Wisdom writers take a divine attribute – God's wisdom – and picture it as a woman. In some of their writings, she is earthy and immediate. But in others she is a heavenly figure, Sophia in the Greek Bible. Sophia is at God's side when the world is created. She guides and nourishes Israel in the wilderness, speaks through the law of Moses and 'pitches her tent' in Jerusalem.[20] In one Wisdom poem she is rejected and even withdraws to heaven:

> Wisdom could not find a place in which she could dwell;
> but a place was found for her in the heavens.
> Then Wisdom went out to dwell with the children of the people,
> but she found no dwelling place.
> So Wisdom returned to her place
> and she settled permanently among the angels.[21]

Sophia's descent and ascent provide the basic theological framework for John's Prologue and his Gospel as a whole.

---

20. Sirach 24:8; the same expression is used of the Word made flesh 'dwelling among us' in John 1:14. Behind both verses is the observation in Exodus 40:34-35 that 'the glory of the LORD' filled the tent of meeting, the portable shrine that the Israelites carried through the wilderness.
21. 1 Enoch 42:1-3, translated by James H. Charlesworth in his The Old Testament Pseudepigrapha, Volume 1, New Haven: Yale University Press, 1983, p. 33.

What are we to make of this wisdom language? Is Sophia a 'real' woman from the heavenly realm? Or is she a poetic way of speaking of God's engagement with the world? By picturing an attribute of God in personal terms, Wisdom writers bridge the gap between the invisible and otherwise unknowable God and everyday human existence. Personifying divine wisdom like this suggests that God is not an abstract principle, like beauty, truth or power. Though God is not a person as we are, the poetry of Sophia suggests that God is not less than personal. Despite all that distinguishes the divine from the realms of time and space, God can be known in his willingness to engage with his creation.

It is not easy to work out where John's Wisdom poem ends. Is it verse 14, or 16 or 18? What is clear is that verses 6-8 and 15 weave into it some lines about John the Baptiser. They certainly disrupt the flow, so much so that some scholars refuse to accept that they were part of the original Prologue. On the other hand, they help to earth John's poetry in the ministry of the first of his witnesses.

I imagine the evangelist recalling how he was drawn to the poetry of Wisdom, through the worship and prayer of his community, and offering what he has written as Sophia's nourishment.

The Evangelist's story

I had been thinking and praying for some time about how to write my account of Jesus. In a quiet moment, when my church had gathered to recall his words and remember him with bread and wine, some lines from the Proverbs of Solomon came into my mind:

Sophia has built her house,
she has mixed her wine,
she has set her table.
'Come, eat of my bread and drink of the wine I have mixed.'

They spoke to me of Jesus, the greatest Wisdom teacher of all. Like Sophia he gives wine and bread, far more than any of us could imagine. His hospitality and the gifts of his table are inexhaustible. My mind went to the Wisdom poems I first read many years ago. So much that they say about Sophia speaks to me of Jesus. She is holy and unique, God's pleasure and delight, the very breath of God's power, the mirror of God's working, the image of God's goodness, the reflection of God's light that will always outshine the darkness of evil. She is there in the story our scriptures tell, right from the very beginning. She reveals God to us. She creates and guides and nourishes God's people. She makes friends with those who receive him, and reaches out even to those who reject him.

'Surely,' I thought, 'Sophia tells the story of Jesus.' So I decided to begin my Gospel with words inspired by her poetry, and weave her images into my work. Of course I had to change her name to Logos, God's Word. But it means the same. Jesus, God's Sophia-Logos, coming down from heaven, taking flesh and blood, pitching his tent in the world, revealing the light of God's glory, returning to live close to the Father's heart. The story of Jesus all seemed to flow from the poetry of God's grace and truth.

How will you read my Prologue, as it introduces my witness to Jesus? Look at its sources, by all means. They certainly inspired me. Change Logos back to Sophia if it helps. But whatever else you do, read my words slowly, and then read them again. Read them with your mind, so that they can shape your thoughts as you read further of Jesus. But read them with your heart too, and let them nourish your spirit so that it soars to the heights and depths of Jesus' presence. Beyond sight and sound and touch he may be, but he is never beyond our reach, forever drawing us into the friendship of the one he called 'Father'.

The beginning of my witness. Our creator's breath-taking Sophia and glory, pitching his tent in flesh and blood. //

How the Evangelist uses his Prologue

John's Prologue introduces his Gospel in three ways. First, it looks backwards, as the evangelist connects the story he is about to tell with all that has gone before, from the very beginning in God's time. The same God who has always been at work in creation and the history of his chosen people is fulfilling his age-old intentions. This new divine initiative centred on Jesus taps into beliefs and hopes that are ancient and enduring: the victory of life and light over darkness and death, God's endless desire to embrace the world despite its indifference and hostility. John's recourse to poetry does not reduce God to a figment of human imagination and abstraction, because 'the Word became flesh and blood, and pitched his tent among us' (1:14). Jesus, we might say, is the body language of God. The story that John tells reveals an initiative that is as human and earthly as it is divine and heavenly.

Secondly, a key theme in the poetry of Sophia-Logos is the movement between earth and heaven. Sophia descends from heaven to earth in order to inhabit the world we know. She ascends back to heaven in 1 Enoch's poem because she is rejected. Descent and ascent are metaphors that speak of the flow of Christ-like grace. As we read further into the Gospel, we will see John using them regularly to suggest that we should read the story he tells at two levels simultaneously. It is the truly human story of Jesus who lives in a particular place and time, with all the constraints that flesh and blood impose. But at the same time this truly human story is the definitive story of God's grace and truth (1:17). The two stories are superimposed onto each other, and the eye of faith brings both into focus.[22]

---

22. On this way of interpreting John's Gospel, see John A. T. Robinson, *The Human Face of God*, SCM Press, 1973, pp. 169-179.

Thirdly, the themes of the Prologue's Wisdom poetry pervade the whole Gospel. As we read further, we will see Jesus fleshing out Wisdom's mission in his teaching and actions, in the impact of his ministry on disciples as well as detractors, and in his promise of the Spirit to come. We may read John's Prologue most often at Christmas, but the Word made flesh is revealed not just in Jesus' birth but throughout his life, and even in his rejection and death. Perhaps this is why, unlike the other Gospels, John has no account of the transfiguration of Jesus on the mountain top, when his earthly appearance is said to shine with God's glory.[23] John presents us with a glory that cannot be confined to one moment or another in the story of Jesus. Wisdom's tent, which houses the radiant presence of God, is pitched across the whole of it.

Reflections

The conclusions of David Csinos' research into different ways of relating to God can help us to reflect on the opening of John's Gospel.[24] Csinos identifies four spiritual styles, different preferences or emphases in the way we experience God. Some people relate best to God through words. They rely on scriptures, written prayers, carefully structured acts of worship, reasoned argument and discussion to draw them near to God. Others come close to God more easily through emotion. Relationships, music and the visual arts, stories and spontaneity help them to grow spiritually. Some people are more symbol-centred. Material objects, icons and other images, poetry and metaphor, the natural world and silence are important in their spirituality. Others experience God more naturally through actions. They find practice more important than theory, and use their faith to make a real difference to the world.

Csinos suggests that as we grow older, our preferences change and we become relatively strong in two or three styles. Healthy churches recognise that spiritual styles vary across the members of their congregations, and leaders take this into account when they plan acts of worship, seasonal activities and programmes that develop faith. Csinos encourages churches to aspire to what he calls 'harmonious dissonance' that nurtures and values people with different spiritual preferences, and incorporates their different approaches to God so that the whole Christian community can flourish.

Set aside some time to reflect on your own relationship with God. Think about where you are, what you are doing, whom you are with, when you feel closest to God. What does this suggest about your spiritual preferences?

---

23. Matthew 17:1-8; Mark 9:2-8; Luke 9:28-36; see also 2 Peter 1:17, 18.
24. See David Csinos, *Children's Ministry That Fits. Beyond One-Size-Fits-All Approaches to Nurturing Children's Spirituality*, Wipf and Stock, 2011. You can find out more about spiritual styles assessments at www.tallpinepress.com. Csinos' approach is used in the lectionary-based learning material published by the ecumenical organisation Roots: see www.rootsontheweb.com.

Read through John's Prologue slowly, and make a note of what catches your attention, what you warm to in its language and imagery, where it speaks most clearly to the way you relate to God. Where do you see reflections of your strongest spiritual styles in John's opening words and ideas? As you read further into the Gospel, look out for more ways in which the story John tells encourages your faith.

Finally, notice where you find John's language off-putting, or where it says less to you. Perhaps here it is reflecting your less preferred spiritual styles back to you. These may represent aspects of Christian faith that you find particularly challenging or uninteresting. Again, as you read through the Gospel, look out for more examples of these and ask what you might do to grow even in these areas of spiritual experience.

TWO

John the Baptist

John 1:19-51

Background

John the Baptist features at the beginning of Jesus' ministry in all four Gospels, though their accounts vary.[25] Mark tells us least. Matthew and Luke include some of John's teaching. These three Gospels have John baptising in the river Jordan, and in Matthew and Mark he is dressed like Elijah the prophet in a leather belt with clothes made from camel's hair, and lives on locusts and wild honey. John's Gospel gives no clues about the Baptist's preaching and call to repentance, and says nothing about his diet and clothing. In John he is active around Bethany beyond the Jordan, where the water came from springs. Interestingly, John includes no record of Jesus' baptism, only a flashback of the Baptist's vision of Jesus. What really matters about John the Baptist to John the Evangelist is his role as a witness to Jesus, hence the lines inserted into the opening poem (1:6-7, 15).

It is only natural that the Jewish authorities should take an interest in the Baptist, though this Gospel plays down his popularity. There is no mention of the crowds who flocked to him from all over Judea and Jerusalem. The enquiry is driven by the Pharisees. It has the feel of an official interrogation and anticipates the nature of the authorities' discussions with Jesus throughout the Gospel. Their questions are informed by popular expectations about the figure who would lead Israel into God's future. Some saw a role for a prophet like Moses (Deuteronomy 18:18), or a revived Elijah, or a messiah (the word means one who is anointed by God's Spirit). Many groups modelled this last figure on David the warrior king, while others saw him as a priest who would renew God's temple. The Baptist keeps his distance from them all, and his repeated 'I am not' provides a sharp contrast with Jesus' 'I am' throughout the Gospel. However his contemporaries imagine the future, John makes it clear that he is not its central figure.

Some writers have wondered whether John was linked with the monastic community at Qumran on the northern shores of the Dead Sea, where the Dead Sea Scrolls were found. The monastery may have been the mother house of a wider renewal movement that spread across Judea and Galilee. The connections between John and the community are tenuous but possible. Both appealed to Isaiah 40:3, which is included in all four Gospel accounts: 'A voice cries out: "In the

---

25. Matthew 3:1-18; Mark 1:2-8; Luke 3:1-18.

wilderness prepare the way of the Lord, make straight in the desert a highway for our God."' And both used water to symbolise the desire for cleansing and renewal. As speculative as these links are, I make something of them as I imagine John's witness to Jesus.

John the Baptist's story

I've always been drawn to the desert, ever since I was a boy. I love the silences. The big skies and open spaces slow me down. They help me clear the clutter and the endless chatter from my head. They speak to me of things I can't put into words – something bigger than 'me' and 'us', something beyond 'here' and 'this', something even more important than finding shelter and the next meal.

It's not just the landscape that draws me to the desert. Our nation was born in a place like this. We found our feet in the wilderness. And now we need a fresh start. Since the Romans invaded our country, we are like slaves on our own soil. So many of us are wondering what the future holds. The prophets say God will come to us again in the desert. Just being out here gives me hope.

I used to belong to the community that lives not far away, on the shores of the Dead Sea. Such a hot, dry spot when the sun is high. So cold and dark at night. An ideal place to escape from the corruption of Jerusalem. The Dead Sea community says that the priests have betrayed us – climbed into bed with Caesar, sold us into slavery, taken us back to captivity. The emperor's man in Syria appoints the high priests now. They collect Rome's taxes and keep the peace or else they send in their troops. Our priests have shopped their own people to a foreign governor. All so that they can hang onto their holy place. Have they forgotten what the prophets said about trusting in the so-called security of the temple?

In the community they pray and eat together, and study the sacred scriptures. They wash their bodies to show that they want to keep their souls clean. We are God's holy place, they say. Out here in the desert, we are getting ready for God to return, as the prophet said we should: 'In the desert prepare the way of the Lord. Make his paths straight'.

I learned a lot in the community, especially about the way God still speaks through the scriptures and calls us to live holy lives. But I wasn't as sure as they were that theirs was the right way to wait for the Lord to come, with all the rules and ritual washings, and the distance they keep from the ordinary people of the land. So after about a year I left. In the community I felt that God was crowded out. Out here in the desert, there is time and space for God. Heaven seems very close.

Some others left the community with me. We live by the water springs, not far from the Jordan. In the spaces and silences, I hear the voice of God.

You prepare the way for me.
You make my paths straight.
You call my people to prepare themselves for my coming.

I send my followers to the towns and villages around here to tell people what we're doing. A lot of them come and see. Some are curious about why we're here. Many of them are hungry and thirsty for God. They want to know how we should live in these unsettling times. They ask what God wants from his people.

Should we take up swords and fight for our freedom from Rome?
Should we do what the priests say and respect our foreign rulers,
    stay loyal to the temple?
Should we live by what the Pharisees say Moses would have us do?
Should we turn our backs on this unclean land and join the
    community in the desert?

So many choices, so many ways. I pray that those who come to me will hear what God is calling me to say. If they do, and they want to change their ways and live for a different kind of world, I baptise them in the living water from the springs.

The authorities from Jerusalem wanted to know what was going on here. I wasn't surprised. They're afraid of trouble.

Who are you?
What gives you the right to tell people how to live?
You're not a priest or a rabbi.
You're not a prophet or the promised one.

I told them it's not me they should be interested in. I'm just a voice. God is calling me to speak about someone far more important. And he's already here with us.

Jesus, the son of Joseph from Nazareth. When I first saw him, I had a vision of the Spirit of God coming to rest on him, like a dove descending from heaven and landing on him. Scriptures came into my mind, and I heard God speaking through them.

This is my Son.
Behold the Lamb of God
who takes away the sin of the world
and leads you to freedom.

Jesus stayed with me for a while. He baptised people with me. But now he's gone home to Galilee. Some of my Galilean followers have gone with him. At first they were drawn to him because he was one of their own. He spoke just like them, he was on their wavelength. But they saw him as much more than a rabbi from Nazareth. 'He's the promised one, the Messiah, the Son of God, the King of Israel,' they told me before they left, like they were repeating my words back to me. They'd got the message. I wonder what the future holds for them.

How John the Evangelist uses the Baptist's story

The evangelist uses his account of John the Baptist and the first appearances of Jesus as a more down-to-earth prologue to the ministry of Jesus than his opening poem. He introduces the Jewish leaders who feature throughout the Gospel. Priests and Levites were associated with the temple, which in Jesus' day was the symbolic centre of the Jewish world. Its architecture spoke of the way Jews understood God's call to be a holy people, with courts that separated Jews from Gentiles, men from women, priests from the rest of the people. Its holiest place (the holy of holies) was accessible only to the high priest, once a year on the Day of Atonement. Its festivals celebrated the stories of the experiences and victories that made God's people what they were. Its daily sacrifices offered opportunities for worship and prayer. The Pharisees were a reform movement in Jesus' day, and he had a lot in common with them. They both rooted their teaching in Scripture. They were both involved in synagogue life. They both stressed the importance of prayer, fasting and almsgiving. They both believed in the resurrection of the dead. The other Gospels reflect something of the diversity of the Pharisaic movement. Some were more liberal than others in their interpretation of Moses, and not all Pharisees were hostile to Jesus. If John wrote his Gospel after the Jewish revolt and the fall of Jerusalem (AD 66–70), the Pharisees were by then the most prominent Jewish group. They appear in this Gospel as a more homogenous body, leading members with the chief priests of the Jewish ruling council (the Sanhedrin), and almost always strongly opposed to Jesus. Whatever their differences, the evangelist unites them in their antipathy towards Jesus.

John goes on to introduce the first followers of Jesus: the brothers Andrew and Simon Peter, Philip and Nathanael. In this Gospel Jesus does not meet Andrew and Simon as Galilean fishermen but as followers of the Baptist. Nathanael is not mentioned in the synoptic Gospels. John has these men coming to faith in Jesus, and confessing him as the Christ, the Son of God and the King of Israel. Notice that Jesus echoes their words by referring to himself as 'the Son of Man' in 1:51, as he does when Peter makes his confession in the synoptics (see Mark 8:29-31 and parallels). There is some overlap in the meaning of these terms in contemporary Jewish writings, where they all refer in different ways to the one whom God will send to liberate his people from slavery and lead them to freedom from their enemies, before establishing his reign in the world, centred on Jerusalem.

The evangelist uses the testimony of the Baptist and the first disciples to define his own understanding of Jesus. John gives his own particular meaning to Jewish terms that the Church had begun to use as titles of Jesus. For example, his 'Christ' (the Greek translation of the Hebrew word 'messiah', which means 'anointed', presumably by God's Spirit) is the one on whom the Baptist sees the Spirit 'remain'. The same word is used of the first disciples' 'staying' or 'remaining' with Jesus in 1:38-42. Later on he speaks of Jesus and the Spirit 'abiding' (same word) in the disciples in 14:17, 23, and Jesus calls them to 'abide' in him in the image of the true vine in chapter 15. According to John, Jesus the Christ is the bearer of the abiding Spirit of God, which his life, death and exaltation will make available to those who are prepared to trust him.

John refers to Jesus as the Christ, the Son of God, the King of Israel and the Son of Man throughout his Gospel. The terms are almost interchangeable, but here in his opening sequence they tell us what John the Baptiser means when he announces that Jesus is 'the Lamb of God who takes away the sin of the world'. Jewish writers did not see the Lamb of God as a sacrificial figure who dealt with sin. For some he was a military figure, a messianic leader. But John the evangelist picks up the ancient association between the Passover lamb and freedom from the time of Moses. He sees the culmination of Jesus' work of liberation in his execution as the true Lamb of God, who dies as the Passover lambs are being slaughtered.[26]

We might compare the account of Jesus' first appearance in the Gospel with the overture to an opera or ballet, in which we can already hear the main themes of the story. It is as if the evangelist is saying: in all that follows, whatever words you want to use about Jesus, whatever titles you give him, he is first and foremost the one who conquers the most destructive powers you can imagine by sacrificing his own life as the supreme revelation of divine love. The end of Jesus' story is here in its beginning. Heaven and earth come together (1:51) as God's Sophia-Logos descends in the flesh and blood of Jesus and ascends in the exaltation of the Lamb of God, to release the renewing power of God's creative Spirit into the whole world.

The evangelist also speaks to those who still follow the Baptist in his day, long after John's death. We know from elsewhere in the New Testament that the Baptist's movement lived on. According to Acts 19:1-7, when Paul was travelling through Ephesus (the traditional setting for the Gospel of John), he met some disciples of Jesus who only knew the baptism of John. John the evangelist appeals to people like them, perhaps on the fringes of his church, to follow the example of their teacher in pledging their loyalty to Jesus. 'He was before me,' says the Baptist, harking back to the Wisdom poetry of the Prologue. John's ministry is over once Jesus appears on the scene. 'He must increase,' he says later to his disciples of Jesus, 'but I must decrease' (3:30). The Baptist may well have been 'a burning and shining lamp', but his glory is eclipsed by the greater testimony of Jesus (5:35, 36).

---

26. I develop this further in the chapter on Joseph of Arimathea on pages 113-118.

Finally, the evangelist sees John the Baptist as the head of a long line of witnesses, many of whom we will hear from as we read through the Gospel. They include Jesus' followers, and people he meets in Galilee, Samaria and Jerusalem, and also Abraham and Moses. Prominent among these witnesses are women like the Samaritan whom Jesus meets by the well, and Mary Magdalene, the first apostle of the resurrection.

Reflections

We can see examples of the spiritual styles described by David Csinos in John the Baptiser's experience of God. There are signs of a spirituality centred on words, emotion, symbols and actions in the references to the scriptures, the open spaces in the wilderness, the symbolism of washing in water and the image of the dove landing and remaining, and the gathering of a community that longed for a different world as it protested against the old one. We can imagine each of these playing their part in opening up John the Baptist to the presence and call of God, and to the coming of Jesus. What do these elements in John's spiritual experience remind you of in yours?

Like all whose faith leads them to leave comforts and securities behind and make their home in the desert, John the Baptist opted for a life on the margins of society to protest against the corruption he saw at the centre of his world. The Baptist's experience reminds us that organisations and institutions – including those associated with religion – are always at risk of allowing factional interests and concerns to become centre-stage. As you reflect on the courage and hope of this marginal figure, and the different people who come to him, who are you reminded of in other times and places, including your own?

1st Sign

The mother of Jesus

John 2:1-12

On the 3rd day there was a wedding...

The good wine until now.

Revealed his glory.

Background

There are no birth stories in John's Gospel. The mother of Jesus (she is never named by the evangelist, unlike her husband at 1:45 and 6:42) only appears at the start of Jesus' ministry in Galilee and at the end by his cross in 19:26. Her presence is alluded to elsewhere, in the exchanges about Jesus' heavenly origins (6:42) and the mention of his brothers (7:1-9). In the heated argument about family connections in 8:31-59, his opponents' riposte 'we were not born of fornication' may hint at rumours that Jesus was. Such insinuations would ensure that in some circles Mary's motherhood was forever shrouded by the lingering memory of shame.

Jesus' relationship with his family elsewhere in the Gospels is ambiguous. Luke shows him as a 12-year-old breaking out of the domestic world governed by his mother, yet still submitting to his parents (Luke 2:41-52). Once his ministry is under way, he becomes an embarrassment to his family (Mark 3:21), and he redefines family in terms of discipleship (Mark 3:31-35), something that John picks up in 19:25-27. In Acts 1:14, Luke notes that Mary and Jesus' brothers are part of the wider family of disciples in Jerusalem waiting for Pentecost.

In Jesus' day, weddings brought together two families, not just two individuals. The celebrations took place in the groom's family home. They involved the whole village, and might last a week. A wedding was an opportunity to display the family's honour to the local community. To cover the costs, close family and friends formed _now_ associations who were obliged to provide food and drink for each other's weddings. Running out of these would seriously damage the family's social standing. _community_

Stone jars were used to store water for the ritual washings prescribed by the law of Moses. Devout people habitually washed hands and eating vessels as a sign of holiness. These practices distinguished them from those who were less devout, and from foreigners who did not recognise the authority of Moses. A house would normally expect to have one of these jars. The presence of six jars suggests that other families in the village had loaned theirs for the occasion.

I imagine Mary helping out at the wedding feast, and finding that the experience of the bridegroom's family reminds her of her own.

Mary's story

It's what every family dreads on an occasion like this. Of course you never know exactly how many people will come, or how much they'll eat and drink, or how long they'll stay for that matter. It's a lot for a family to provide on their own. I've known this family for years. Ever since our children were young and our husbands worked together building houses for the new Roman settlers in Galilee. We used to live quite close together until they moved to Cana, not too far from where my family still lives in Nazareth. This is the first time I've been to Cana. And the first wedding I've been invited to since my husband Joseph died two years ago. Thankfully, Jesus and my other sons are with me, so I don't feel quite so alone.

Celebrations like this can last for days. Eating and drinking, music and dancing. And lots of catching up, telling stories, meeting old friends and making new ones. Some of Jesus' friends are here too. They come from much further away – the other side of Galilee, by the lake. A couple of them are fishermen, though he told me he met them in Judea, when they all lived out in the desert with John the baptiser. Not much to eat and drink there, not like today at this feast.

I'm helping out with the catering. That's how I know the wine has run out. The shame of it. It's not hard to guess what's going through everyone's minds, despite eating and drinking themselves stupid. I can hear them muttering to each other. 'What kind of a father is it who can't provide enough for his son's wedding feast?' 'Their friends can't think much of them if they don't give them enough wine for the wedding feast.'

I feel for the family. I know about shame. I remember how my father and mother felt when I was carrying Jesus. So young, not yet married. I remember being sent away to live with relatives in Judea until the dust settled. Not that it ever did, not fully. Even to this day in Nazareth, some people keep their distance because of what happened all those years ago. They have long memories round here. Shame lingers.

I've told Jesus about the wine. He's a good friend of the groom. He won't want to see this family humiliated. I'm sure he'll do the right thing and send the servants out to buy more. He didn't seem very enthusiastic about helping, though. But I can see him now, having a word with the servants. I wonder why they're filling the water jars. That will take ages. Now they're taking some of the water to the steward. Why on earth are they doing that? Surely they don't think he's so drunk that he won't notice! He's tasting it, and he seems to like it. Whatever it is, it must be good – he's praising the bridegroom sky high.

I knew Jesus would help out. But I can't work out what he did. Water from the big stone jars . . . the best wine at the wedding? Whatever he's done, he's saved this family's honour.

How John uses the story of the wedding feast

John gives some strong hints about the way he uses this story in his references to time. His opening words set the wedding feast 'on the third day', linking it with what happens on the third day after Jesus' crucifixion. It is also the seventh day since the beginning of John the Baptiser's testimony (see the references to 'the next day' in 1:29, 35, 43), which suggests that this third day is also a kind of sabbath, when the baptiser's work of bearing witness is fulfilled. Jesus responds to his mother's request by telling her that his 'hour' has not yet come. That has to wait for his passion, death and resurrection, when his 'glory' is fully revealed (13:1, 31, 32; 17:1). These references to Jesus' hour and glory suggest that the events at the wedding feast point beyond themselves to something greater, Jesus' return to his heavenly glory through the death that exalts him to heaven and releases God's gift of the transforming Spirit.

Hints of Jesus' exaltation remind us of the ascent of Sophia, and there are strong Wisdom themes in this story. Jesus' mother knows who to approach when the wine runs out. She reminds us of the disciples of Sophia, who trust her as the source of wine and bread. John presents her as a woman of initiative, a true disciple of Jesus and not merely his mother. She directs us to her son, in whom the fullness of Sophia-Logos is found. Abundant wine (150 gallons would fill close to 500 bottles) is typical of Sophia's generous provision, and points forward to the abundance of bread and fish around the Sea of Tiberias later in the Gospel.

The Bible uses wine as a symbol of victory and hope. In Isaiah 25:6-8, God provides only the finest wine at the feast that celebrates the defeat of his enemies. Joel 3:18 and Amos 9:13, 14 expect the mountains to drip sweet wine in God's glorious future. In popular mythology the Greek god Dionysius also turned water into wine, and in John's world there were numerous legends of springs miraculously producing wine.

The story of Jesus turning water into wine can be seen as a parable of the transforming presence of the risen Christ. He turns the possibility of shame for the family of the bridegroom into honour. They have kept the best wine until now, a typical piece of Johannine irony in which the steward says more than he realises. Jesus transforms something quite ordinary – which the law of Moses uses to order the world into what is clean and unclean – into a means of grace and blessing. Intimations of the Eucharist in the story remind us that sacramental grace also transforms the ordinary taking and sharing of bread and wine. As a glimpse of the glory to come, this first in a series of signs lays the foundations of hope for a better world, in which poor disabled outcasts are healed, the hungry are fed and the powers of death are finally defeated.[27]

---

27. John's seven signs are the changing of water into wine (2:1-11), the healing of the centurion's son (4:46-54), the healing of the paralysed man (5:1-18), the feeding of the five thousand (6:1-15), Jesus' walking on the water (6:16-21), the healing of the man born blind (9:1-41) and the raising of Lazarus (11:1-44).

Reflections

The story of the wedding feast is set in the everyday world of family, community and celebration. In the introduction to the Church of England's latest Marriage Service, Jesus' presence at the wedding in Cana is said to be a sign of his presence at all weddings.[28] We might want to go further. If we are right in seeing the story as a parable of the transforming presence of Christ, perhaps it can encourage us to look out for his presence wherever people experience shame, or long to be able to celebrate a better life and a better world.

As you look at your world, what alerts you to the presence of Christ in situations of humiliation and hope? What difference can you and other people of faith make to them?

Think about the role of Jesus' mother in the story. Her initiative in the face of a domestic and social crisis reminds us of the disciples of Sophia who know where God's abundant generosity lies. How does the example of Jesus' mother encourage you to respond to a particular example of need or crisis in your world, knowing what you do about Jesus as the one who transforms even the most meagre resources into rich springs of God's blessing? *Rowan Williams*

REFUGEES — CHANNEL ISLANDS
HOMELESS
JACK ELLISON

IAN FORSTER
MIKE WILLIAMS

---

28. In The Archbishops' Council, *Common Worship: Pastoral Services*, London: Church House Publishing, 2005.

FOUR

Nicodemus
John 3:1-21

Background

The story of Jesus' meeting with Nicodemus the Pharisee reminds us of his encounters with Jewish officials in the other Gospels. In Luke 10:25-37, he has a conversation with a lawyer about the implications of the coming of God's kingdom for life in the present world. In Mark 12:28-34, he has a similar discussion with a scribe who wants to know which of the more than 600 laws associated with Moses is the most important. The scribe is wise enough to concur with Jesus' judgement, and Jesus tells him that he is 'not far from the kingdom of God'.

The lawyer and the scribe may have been Pharisees, though Luke and Mark do not say as much. They certainly share the Pharisees' interest in the coming of God's kingdom, which is a major theme in Jesus' teaching in the other Gospels (Matthew prefers to use an equivalent, 'the kingdom of heaven'). The expression refers to God's reign or rule, rather than a territory. Popular expectation at the time of Jesus held that God's reign over the world was real though hidden, not least because God's chosen people had been under foreign rule for centuries. The arrival of God's kingdom would remove all traces of doubt as to his sovereignty, and faithful Israelites would at last enjoy God's long-promised blessings. When Jesus speaks of God's kingdom he claims that God's future is already taking shape in his teaching and activity.

The term 'kingdom of God' only occurs twice in this Gospel, both times in this story. John prefers the equivalent term 'eternal life', which is not 'life after death' as the Authorised Version's translation 'everlasting life' implies, but 'life in the age to come', when God's reign finally appears.[29] This Gospel emphasises eternal life as a present reality available to those who put their faith in Jesus, yet without completely losing sight of its future, as the references to 'the last day' in 5:25 and 11:25, 26 show.

John's account of the meeting between Jesus and the prominent Pharisee Nicodemus about what it means to experience the kingdom of God is more detailed than anything like it in the other Gospels. As we shall see, it explores issues that were not only of concern to Jesus' audience, but also to that of the evangelist.

---

29. In Mark 10:17-27, Jesus' conversation with the rich man, and subsequently with his disciples, uses the terms interchangeably.

I imagine Nicodemus troubled by the challenges of being God's holy people under the Roman occupation as he remembers the glory of the Torah and the temple. Troubled too by Jesus and the impact his ministry is having on the synagogue he leads.

Nicodemus' story

I am a leader of the synagogue and a teacher of the Torah, the very word of God. Torah tells us that God made the world, and gave Moses his commandments to teach us how to live. We learn so much from Moses – how to worship God, how to pray, how to celebrate our great festivals like the Passover, how to make sure that God's world is just, how to live our everyday lives. I study the Torah constantly so that I can hear God's voice speaking today, like he did to Moses. And I want to teach others to do the same, so that we can live holy lives because, as scripture says, the Lord our God is holy.

But how are we to be God's holy people today? Moses gave us more than 600 commandments. Some rabbis say they can be summed up in just two. We are to love God with all our heart and mind and soul and strength, and our neighbour as ourselves. If only it were that simple! Life today is so complicated. How do we keep ourselves holy when there is so much temptation in the world, so much that contaminates our lives? Our homeland is no longer our own. The Romans have been here for nearly a hundred years. We see their footprints everywhere, on their roads and buildings and coins stamped with the emperor's head. They even say he is a god! It is impossible to avoid the impurity they bring. So we have to pay very careful attention to Moses if we are to live pure and holy lives, as God expects. We must keep the Sabbath, because it reminds us that God is special and we are special. We must avoid unclean foods and practices. We must purify ourselves daily. We must follow the example of Abraham and circumcise our boys. All these things show how devoted we are to God, how different we are from other nations and how determined we are to keep ourselves from falling into foreign ways.

The synagogue is my world. Every day people from our community come together there around the scriptures. We worship and pray and hear the word of God at the same time as the priests offer sacrifices in the temple in Jerusalem. The Sabbath is our most important day. All work stops. The whole community gathers. We eat together, worship together, pray together, study together. The true temple, of course, is in heaven. God showed Moses what it looks like. Awe-inspiring as it is, our holy place on Mount Zion is but a copy of the heavenly shrine. So when we worship and pray on earth, in the synagogue or in the temple, the curtain is drawn back and we're in heaven with the angels and the holy ones who have gone before us, worshipping the God of Israel, the Lord of all creation. Blessed be the God of Abraham, Isaac and Jacob forever!

But our synagogue has recently been disturbed. Jesus the son of Joseph, a rabbi from Galilee, attended our services for a while, and some of us are impressed by him. He has no formal training in the Torah, but he brings the scriptures to life before our eyes. Who can doubt his passion for the God of our fathers? Who can question his compassion when he stretches out his hands to heal the sick? When he teaches or prays, it is like hearing the voice of one of the prophets. He speaks of the coming of a new world, the kingdom of God. He sees the Spirit of God blowing new life into creation, like God breathed life into Adam. He says our nation needs a new beginning from God, like being born over again. Such an inspiration! But not everyone is impressed.

You see, for all his holiness Jesus isn't strict about keeping the Sabbath. 'God is always working to bring life,' he says, 'and I am sent to do God's work, even if that means healing a man on the Sabbath.' People ask me, 'What does he mean? Does God really want us to disregard what he said through Moses?' They are afraid that if we do not keep the Sabbath, we will be like everyone else – children of Caesar, rather than the offspring of Abraham and Moses.

Our synagogue is divided. Some would be happy to stone him for blasphemy. 'Where does he get his authority from?' they say. 'He is the son of a carpenter from Nazareth. He speaks with the devil's tongue.' But others among us dare to think that he might be the expected one, the prophet promised by Moses, or even the messiah himself. His supporters say, 'What more are we to expect from the anointed one when he comes?'

What am I to do, as a leader of our people? I have decided to speak with the rabbi Jesus, to ask him about the signs he does and the kingdom he speaks of. At present he is staying not far from here. I will go to him when it is safe, after dark, when no one will see me. I hope he will answer my questions. And help me to heal the divisions in our community.

How John uses the story of Nicodemus

Jesus' conversation with Nicodemus is taking place on two levels. On the face of it, Jesus has a secret, late-night meeting with a prominent Jewish leader who seeks him out because of what he sees in Jesus' ministry. Nicodemus struggles to understand Jesus' earthy and self-evidently biblical talk of birth and the Spirit, but in true Johannine fashion, his difficulties serve to draw out what Jesus really means, and we may assume that he leaves in a more enlightened state than he arrived.

But this is also a conversation between two communities. In verse 2, Nicodemus speaks as a representative: 'Rabbi, *we know* that you are a teacher who has come from God.' In verse 7, Jesus addresses his synagogue: '*You* (plural) must be born from above.' In verse 11, Jesus also speaks as a representative, to Nicodemus' community: '*we speak* of what we know . . . yet you (plural) do not receive our testimony'.

What is happening here? John does not seem to be simply reporting Jesus' meeting with Nicodemus, but using it to appeal to people from Nicodemus' world. At least some of them believe in Jesus to a point. The signs of healing they have seen in Jerusalem lead them to conclude that Jesus has come from God, and that God is in some sense with him. But Jesus is not prepared to trust this kind of response (2:24). It lacks something.

Jesus speaks about birth as a way of seeing or entering into the experience of God's reign. This reminds us of his teaching in Mark 10:15 about receiving God's kingdom like a little child as the only way to enter it. In both cases, Jesus speaks metaphorically. At first Nicodemus interprets what he hears literally. Jesus is deliberately ambiguous. He talks about being born 'from above', but the Greek can also mean 'again', which is how Nicodemus hears him. Jesus tries to overcome his misunderstanding by explaining what his birth metaphor means. To be born 'from above' is to be born 'of water and Spirit', or later, to be born 'of Spirit'. This takes John's audience back to his Prologue, with its talk of those who welcome Jesus by believing in him becoming 'children of God' who are 'born of God' (1:12, 13).

Nicodemus, the leading teacher of Israel, is baffled by Jesus' talk of a mysterious birth. John's audience understands that Jesus is speaking of baptism, when believers make a public statement of their faith in Jesus and join the community of his brothers and sisters. Jesus is telling those whom Nicodemus represents that it is not enough to be impressed by his works of healing and the teaching that accompanies them. If they really are serious about engaging with the God who sent him and the kingdom that is beginning to take shape around him, they must be courageous enough to come out of the shadows and be baptised.

That will have consequences. The story of the healing of the man born blind in chapter 9, and the words of Jesus to his disciples before his death in chapter 16 make it clear that relations between church and synagogue in John's world are strained, to say the least. If they make their faith in Jesus public, Nicodemus' people will be standing with those whom their synagogue has marginalised and victimised. Such solidarity will be costly. They and their families are likely to be ostracised by their own people. What can empower Nicodemus and those in the synagogue who like him are sympathetic to Jesus, but not courageous enough to come out of the shadows?

As the conversation proceeds, Nicodemus seems to recede further into the darkness, and Jesus comes to the fore to testify to the full Johannine faith in the descending and ascending heavenly one. John's audience recognises the poetry of Sophia-Logos from the Prologue, though here the talk is of 'the Son of Man'. John 1:51, with its allusions to the story of Jacob's dream at Bethel in Genesis 28:12, uses this expression to picture Jesus the living link between earth and heaven. His descent from heaven is God's costly act of generous love, of which the story of Abraham's willingness to sacrifice Isaac his son in Genesis 22 is a mere hint. The Son of Man's ascent is like Moses lifting up the bronze serpent in the wilderness in Numbers 21:4-9, to relieve those who were bitten by poisonous snakes, though in 12:32, the benefits of the Son of Man's ascent are eternal and universal.

By the time we reach verse 16, it is not clear whether Jesus or the evangelist is speaking. It hardly matters as far as the message to Nicodemus and the sympathisers in the synagogue is concerned. The coming of Jesus as the flesh-and-blood dwelling place of Sophia-Logos faces 'you' with a stark choice. Either you go public by being baptised, and come into the light and life of the one who brings heaven and earth together; or you stay in the dark and live with the judgement that is the shadow-side of divine love.

There are no half measures, says the evangelist. There is no safety in the shadows, because the darkness can only obscure God's desire to bring the whole world to life. Paradoxically, wholeness only comes through division. 'You' who are drawn to Jesus must choose between being born into a life that is earth-bound or heavenly, between unbelief or faith, darkness or light, judgement or abundant life.

Faced with any kind of choice, people look for examples who reflect their options back to them. The evangelist could hardly be more forthcoming about the authority of Jesus and the response he looks for. But what about Nicodemus? What kind of role model is he? He appears twice more in the Gospel. In 7:50, he stands up to the chief priests and Pharisees by insisting that they give Jesus a hearing. In 19:38-42, he and Joseph of Arimathea, another secret disciple, procure Jesus' body, anoint it with a quantity of spices fit for a king and then bury it – all after nightfall. Does Nicodemus' undoubted boldness suggest that he has finally come into the light by the end of the story? Or, as some suggest, does his desire to hang onto his honour as a leader of the Jews (see 12:42, 43) mean that he is still in the dark, no further along the road to faith than honouring the dead body of Jesus?

Reflections

Jesus' images of birth and Spirit (the Hebrew word *ruach* is translated as 'spirit' or 'breath' in the Bible) remind us that a newly-born child's first breath is a sure sign of life, as well as a great relief to all who are involved in the birth. Imagine your own faith as a kind of birth, in which you are animated by the breath of God. How would you describe the family of faith that you have been born into? How does your membership of this family strengthen your solidarity with those who are oppressed because of their faith, Christian and otherwise?

In the Introduction, I suggested some reasons why John the evangelist uses the black-and-white, either/or language that we find in his account of Jesus and Nicodemus. It reflects the real-world experience of his audience. When they heard language like this, they would have had particular people and communities in mind. Who do you think about when you read this story, with its sharp boundaries and stark choices? ✗ What would you say to John the evangelist when you consider what you know of people who do not fit into his black and white categories?

✗ THE TALISMAN —
CERTAINTY HUNTING.
MY DESIRE TO BE IN AN EXCLUSIVE GROUP
DISTANCING MYSELF FROM THOSE
I DISAGREE WITH OR DON'T LIKE

FIVE

The Samaritan woman

John 4:1-42   /—/5

Background

The Samaritans lived in the region of Samaria, 40 miles north of Jerusalem and the former capital of the northern kingdom of Israel. Often called Ephraim in the Bible, Israel was associated with the patriarch Jacob and his favourite son Joseph. Samaria was founded by King Omri in about 880 BC. His son Ahab expanded it into a wealthy and powerful centre. Evidence from the Bible and archaeology suggests that Samaria hosted the worship of Yahweh alongside the Canaanite gods Baal and Asherah, which drew considerable criticism from the prophets. The Assyrians captured Samaria in 721 BC, deported much of the population and re-settled the city with foreigners (2 Kings 17:6, 24-41). In the post-Assyrian period, Yahweh worshippers established their own temple on Mount Gerizim, independent of Jerusalem, and translated the books of Moses. They expected a messiah, the Taheb, who would be a teacher sent from God.

Jews regarded Samaritans as foreigners, and treated them with contempt. They destroyed the Samaritan temple in 128 BC, which was the main reason for the antipathy that persisted in Jesus' day. Jews were encouraged to avoid Samaritans, and regarded their women as being in a permanent state of menstrual uncleanness. Luke 9:51-55 tells of a Samaritan village that refused hospitality to Jesus and his disciples. But his next chapter includes one of Jesus' best-known parables, whose hero is a Samaritan (Luke 10:30-37).

In Acts 8, Samaria was an early centre of Christian mission, following the martyrdom of Stephen and the subsequent persecution of the church in Jerusalem. Philip, one of the deacons appointed with Stephen, had a particularly successful ministry there. The spread of the gospel to Samaria was a significant part of its expansion beyond Judea and Galilee to 'the ends of the earth' (Acts 1:8).

Though the Bible says nothing about Jacob owning a well, he would no doubt have dug one on the land he bought in Shechem (Genesis 33:18-20), which was probably the Sychar of this story. A village well was a public place. The early books of the Bible include a number of stories of well-side meetings with future wives. In Genesis 24, the well is where Abraham's servant meets Rebekah, who later becomes Isaac's wife. In Genesis 29, Jacob meets Rachel when she comes to water her father's sheep. In Exodus 2, the seven daughters of Jethro, the priest of Midian, are also watering their flocks when Moses meets them, and Jethro rewards him for his kindness by giving one of them, Zipporah, to him as his wife. The marriage theme in these stories surfaces in John's account, when Jesus asks the Samaritan woman about her husbands.

The Samaritan woman belonged to a world in which women chiefly inhabited the private world of the home, and carried out domestic roles that included collecting water. Honourable women behaved so as not to provoke public comment. This included not speaking with men outside the family away from the home. In some ways the woman Jesus meets by the well is bound by contemporary social conventions, but in others she steps outside them.

I imagine the Samaritan woman speaking about her surprising meeting with a Jewish man Jesus, and the way their conversation started to enlarge her horizons.

The Samaritan woman's story

Every day's the same. I get up at the crack of dawn. Before anyone else is awake I knead dough for the daily bread. Then I get the oven ready for the day's cooking. I eat some of yesterday's bread if there's any left. Then when the men are up and gone, I clean the house. Same thing every day. It's my job to collect the water. It isn't far to walk to the well in the town square, but the journey back, carrying all that water, makes it seem miles away. If I was a decent woman like the others round here, I'd be able to go to the well early with them, before the sun gets high. But I'm not a decent woman, not in their eyes anyway. They turn their backs and talk about me. They treat me like something they'd rather not tread on. What are they afraid of? Do they think they'll catch something from me – just because I'm not married to the man I live with? I'm not ashamed to be his mistress. At least I don't sell my body for a living.

I remember a very hot day last week. Usually there's no one in the square when I arrive – that's why I go so late. But there was a man sitting there all alone, as if he was waiting for someone. As I drew the water and started to fill my jar, he spoke to me. Decent men and women never speak to one another in public, only at home, but he asked me for a drink. I knew straightaway, I could tell from his accent, that he wasn't one of us. He was a Galilean. One of their people. They don't like us and we don't like them. And as for sharing each other's food and drink, that's unthinkable.

Why did he speak to me? What was he after? I asked him straight: 'why do you want water from me?' I couldn't make out what he was saying. He started talking about me asking him for water. He said that if I knew who he was, I'd be asking him for water, but not from a well. Spring water, living water. I had no idea how he was going to get it, but anything to save making this journey every day. Then he changed the subject. 'Go and get your husband,' he said. I remembered the story

of our father Jacob meeting his future wife Rachel by the well. And I thought to myself, 'I hope he's got nothing like that in mind. I may only be a mistress but I'm proud to be a Samaritan. I'm not so desperate that I'd want to marry one of their people!'

How did he know I'm not married? Did I let something slip? Not that I'm ashamed, like I said. That's just the way others in the village see me. It didn't seem to bother him. 'You're a prophet,' I said. I just blurted it out, without really thinking. 'If you're one of their people, talking to a shameful woman like me, perhaps you can settle one of the old scores that has divided my people from yours for ages.' I asked him about the temple. 'Yours or ours – which is the right place to worship God? Which mountain is closer to heaven – Gerizim or Zion?' I was amazed at his answer. 'Neither.' I was ready to go for him when he started talking down at me, like a typical man from Jerusalem: 'unlike us, you don't know what you're worshipping'. What an insult! But his next words completely threw me. 'God is spirit, and he wants people to worship him as their heavenly Father, in spirit and truth not in temples made with hands.'

I never imagined one of them talking like that. 'Perhaps this is the prophet Moses spoke about, even the messiah we Samaritans are expecting, the one who'll teach us the truth.' He seemed to say as much. Then a group of men arrived. I could tell they were Galileans. They made such a fuss about him talking to a woman. What a surprise! Time to go. But I couldn't keep quiet about the man I'd just been speaking to. I ran off and left my water jar behind – I could get that later. I forgot all about what they think of me in the town. I told everyone I saw there about the Galilean man I'd been speaking to – I didn't even know his name at the time – and how he knew all about me, and what he'd said about God and spirit and living water and temples. I can't have made much sense, but a group of our men went to the square, and spoke with him and his friends. They even invited him to break his journey and stay with us for a couple of days. Can you imagine – a group of their people staying with us, like he did with me, sharing each other's food and drink?

My world has just got bigger. ⫽

How John uses the Samaritan woman's story

John uses the story of Jesus and the Samaritan woman to address those on the margins of the Jewish world, just as he used the Nicodemus narrative to appeal to those in the synagogue. As a centre of the Jesus movement in a world despised by the Jewish mainstream, disciples there could easily feel disadvantaged by their historical and racial heritage. By associating their origins with a Samaritan woman commended by Jesus, John assures them – and reminds those who continue to despise them – of their honoured place in the people who are born of God.

The narrative is not so much a report of an actual conversation as a carefully constructed account that shows some similarities with the later stories of Jesus healing the blind man in chapter 9 and raising Lazarus in chapter 11. Unlike them, however, it conveys a greater impression of movement. Jesus is travelling north, from Judea to Galilee, to avoid the attention of the Pharisees following the success of his ministry. He and his disciples break their journey in Sychar, a Samaritan town, where he meets a woman who has left her home to draw water from the town's well. The disciples go into the town to buy food. When they return, the woman goes into the town to tell its people about Jesus. Then some of them come to Jesus, and persuade him to stay with them. Eventually after two days Jesus and his disciples resume their journey, and we next meet him in Cana. These movements suggest that Jesus' mission too is on the move, putting pressure on significant boundaries in his world, most obviously those around gender and race. Though Jesus is still operating within the broad family of Israel, there are hints in the story that his mission has even wider horizons in view.

We have read enough of the Gospel by now to recognise some of its typical features in Jesus' conversation with the woman. She misunderstands Jesus at first, though like the men Jesus meets among the disciples of John the Baptiser, she eventually makes a confession of faith. She takes his promise of living water literally, just as Nicodemus did when Jesus spoke about birth. There is irony in the way she asks Jesus if he is greater than the patriarch Jacob. John's audience can provide the answer. As the embodiment of Sophia-Logos, Jesus 'was' before Jacob, just as he 'was' before John the Baptiser. He will shortly reveal that he was before Abraham too (8:58).

The woman's misunderstanding, like that of Nicodemus, opens up new levels of meaning in Jesus' words. He has not come to do away with the domestic division of labour, but to fulfil Sophia's offer of the water of heavenly revelation in Sirach 24:21, not simply through his teaching but supremely in his sacrificial death. In one of the ceremonies at the festival of Booths later in the Gospel, as water from the pool of Siloam is being poured out in the temple, he will issue Sophia's invitation: 'Let anyone who is thirsty come to me, and let the one who believes in me drink. As the scripture has said, "Out of his heart shall flow rivers of living water"' (7:37, 38). Only John refers to the water that flows with blood from the side of the crucified Jesus (19:34). 'Living water' from the heart of Jesus symbolises the Holy Spirit, the gift of the glorified Lord to his disciples (14:15-31; 20:22) and his continuing presence in the world through them.[30]

---

30. I assume that the 'heart' referred to in 7:38 belongs to Jesus, not to the believer. This seems to make more sense of the cross references within John's Gospel as a whole. The English translations vary. The RSV retains the ambiguity, but the NRSV closes it down, with its translation, 'out of the believer's heart shall flow rivers of living water'.

The story also has some distinctive features. The Samaritan woman is a marginal figure in more ways than one. In patriarchal Jewish eyes, she is defined negatively by her race and gender. She is probably ostracised by her own community too on account of her colourful history with men. The narrative explores the implications of her faith. As a woman, her feisty conversation with Jesus and her initiative in telling others from her community about Jesus remind us of the mother of Jesus earlier at the wedding in Cana, and of Mary Magdalene towards the end of the Gospel, when she tells the disciples that she has seen the risen Jesus (20:18). Unlike Nicodemus the high-ranking teacher of Israel, this low-status anonymous woman is a true disciple. Her testimony shows how Jesus, the embodiment of God's Sophia-Logos and all-embracing love (3:16), breaks through some of the most significant barriers in his world, to create a community of those who are born 'not of blood . . . but of God' (1:13).

John is interested in showing how the woman's faith in Jesus develops. When she first meets Jesus, she sees him in the light of her racial and gender stereotypes, as a tired, hungry Jewish man who should not be speaking to her in public. Despite all that they have in common as descendants of Jacob, Jesus draws attention to what divides them. She does not know 'the gift of God' (that is, the Jewish scriptures), which regularly use water to symbolise God. He goes on to tell her that she and her people do not know the God they worship on their holy mountain (verse 22; he says the same of the Pharisees in 8:19). But as their conversation moves from the domestic realm into more personal areas, she becomes more spiritually alert and starts to move across the barriers they both stand behind. She wonders whether he might be a prophet, and so she asks him about the most important issue that divides them: 'whose temple is truly God's dwelling place – yours or ours?'

Her question draws Jesus to say more about something he mentioned earlier in the Gospel, in Jerusalem, when he called time on the temple there. 'Destroy this temple, and in three days I will raise it up' (2:19) refers not to an alternative structure to the one that Herod was renovating at the time, but to his own broken and exalted body. What was he saying about true worship? He tells her that this has nothing to do with particular peoples guarding contested sites on allegedly holy mountains like Zion and Gerizim. Instead, true worship reflects the reality of God who, as 'Spirit', refuses to be defined by 'blood or the will of the flesh or the will of man' (1:13). Jesus refuses to endorse anyone's holy places, because true worship is a reflection of relationship not place, however holy. God's true temple is where Sophia-Logos pitches her tent and radiates her glory (1:14). True worshippers are not those who are born Jews or Samaritans, but of God, from above, of the Spirit.

This is heady stuff, and it takes the determined Samaritan woman still further. She wonders whether Jesus might be the Samaritans' messiah, the expected teacher from God. 'Much more,' is the gist of Jesus' reply: '"I am", the embodiment of Sophia-Logos, is speaking to you.' At this, she abandons her water jar and sets off for the town to invite her people to 'come and see'. These words in verse 29 are a typical Johannine invitation to discipleship. What John's audience sees is the woman's emerging faith in Jesus empowering her to cross the boundaries that enclose her world, as a despised Samaritan woman whose people do not really know the God they worship.

The clarity of her faith throws the returning disciples' bemusement into sharp relief. They are puzzled, not only by Jesus' speaking with a woman in public but by his mystifying talk of food (4:31-34). The most obvious, literal meaning confuses them. But as a metaphor for 'doing the will of God', it leads into the parable of the harvest as a picture of the mission that is taking shape in Samaria. Jesus the sower is collapsing the usual interval between sowing and reaping. He invites his disciples to set aside their confusion and see themselves as reapers who will celebrate the fruits of his labour with him.

The woman may have a bad reputation locally, but her testimony to Jesus is credible enough to draw many from her town to him. Like John the Baptiser, she has now done her work of paving the way for Jesus to speak for himself. By asking him to 'stay' (the Greek *menein* is translated elsewhere in the Gospel as 'remain' and 'abide', and is strongly associated with discipleship), the Samaritans reveal their desire to become his disciples, like the Galileans Philip, Andrew, Simon and Nathanael (1:38-51). Their confession of faith in Jesus as 'Saviour of the world' signifies the movement outwards, from Judea and Galilee to Samaria and beyond. Jesus is already beginning to draw the whole world to himself (12:32).

Reflections

The story of Jesus and the Samaritan woman shows him in dialogue with a woman from a race whom his own people thought of as inferior. Even her own community would have treated her with some caution. Jesus teaches her as much about herself as himself. I wonder whether John gives her story so much space because he wants his audience to learn from this anonymous, marginal woman. What impresses and inspires you most about her? What do you think you can learn from her as a woman, a believer and a human being?

People in contemporary western societies often make the distinction between 'spirituality' and 'religion'. It seems that many more are interested in finding meaning and purpose in life than in belonging to faith communities and religious bodies. Yet the relationship between the two is often more complex. Many people find it impossible to be spiritual without also being religious.[31] How much do you see Jesus' attitude to holy places and his understanding of God as 'Spirit' as evidence of his understanding of the relationship between spirituality and religion? If you think of yourself as religious, where do you find Jesus spiritually challenging?

HONESTY
DIRECTNESS
NO SYCOPHANCY
BUT ATTRACTION

A 'HOLY PLACE' IS A STARTING
GROUND.
WE GO IN IN ORDER TO LEAVE.

---

31. See Paul Heelas and Linda Woodhead, *The Spiritual Revolution. Why Religion is Giving Way to Spirituality*, Oxford: Blackwell Publishing, 2005; Philip Sheldrake, *Spirituality. A Very Short Introduction*, Oxford: Oxford University Press, 2012; Christopher Jamison, *Finding Sanctuary. Monastic Steps for Everyday Life*, London: Weidenfeld and Nicolson, 2006.

SIX

The royal official
John 4:46-54

Background

Stories of Jesus' healing ministry occur throughout the Gospels. In most of them he cured diseases or disabling conditions such as blindness, deafness and paralysis. He also expelled evil spirits (though not in John's Gospel), and in a very small number of cases raised the dead (the raising of Lazarus in John 11 is the longest and most spectacular of these accounts in the Gospels). Sometimes Jesus used the methods of traditional healers, such as touch or anointing with spittle or mud paste (Mark 1:41; 7:33; John 9:6). Often his word was sufficient. Like his contemporaries, Jesus acknowledges some connection between sickness and sin, without admitting a direct link (Mark 2:5; John 5:14; 9:3). According to the Gospels, there was no disputing his power to heal, only its source, which his detractors insisted was diabolical rather than divine (Mark 2:1-10; 3:20-27).

There are two other stories in the Gospels similar to John's account of the healing of the royal official's son. Matthew 8:5-13 is virtually the same as the account in Luke 7:1-10. Both have a Gentile centurion in Capernaum who is very concerned about his slave's serious illness, but some of the details differ. Where Matthew has the centurion approaching Jesus directly about a slave who is paralysed and in great distress, Luke has local Jewish elders interceding with Jesus on behalf of a man who has been very generous towards their community, and whose slave is close to death. Matthew includes a saying that compares this Gentile's faith with those who will come from all over the world to eat and drink with the patriarchs when God's kingdom comes. Luke has similar words elsewhere in his Gospel (13:28, 29).

In John's account, the man is a described as a royal official, and it is his son rather than his slave who is ill. He may have worked for Herod Antipas, the Romans' puppet king in Galilee at the time, as what we now call a civil servant. Alternatively, he could have been a member of the royal family, as I assume when I have him tell his story. Unlike the centurion in Matthew and Luke, he lives in Cana, 20 miles to the west of Capernaum. Like Matthew's centurion he speaks to Jesus directly, but receives a less than welcoming response. Jesus' apparently dismissive remarks in verse 48 associate the official with others from Galilee who are drawn to him by his reputation as a healer. He is reluctant to trust such people (see 2:24) and sends him away, perhaps to test the sincerity of his faith.

In none of the accounts does Jesus get to meet the sick person. They all show him healing at a distance, though in Luke and Matthew both Jesus and the sick slave are in Capernaum, to highlight faith in the authority of Jesus' word. This is where John's interest lies, and he magnifies the distance between healer and healed by having the son in Capernaum and Jesus in Cana. Even when Jesus is far away, John assures his audience that his word is powerful.

I imagine the royal official recounting the struggle he had to see beyond his prejudices and trust Jesus the healer from Nazareth with his son's life.

The royal official's story

I hope you realise that this isn't how someone with my background would normally behave. I'm wealthy, well connected and highly regarded. In the circles I move in, people wouldn't dream of asking favours of anyone from Nazareth. Everybody knows that nothing good comes out of that place. But I asked Jesus of Nazareth for help. No, more than that, I begged him to come and heal my son.

I had no option. My boy had been ill for about a week. He had a fever. He would sweat and then go cold. There was no end to it. Nothing we could do made the slightest difference. I brought in the best doctors that money could buy, and they couldn't do anything either. My son's life was slipping away. It was all we could do to make him feel comfortable.

One of my slaves told me about Jesus, a rabbi from Nazareth, who was back in Cana. There are stories there about the way he saved a family's reputation. The wine ran out at their son's wedding. He told them to serve water, and it tasted like the finest wine. According to my slave, he's a healer too. Some of the locals have seen him in Jerusalem. They say it doesn't matter who you are, he always has a good word and a kind action.

I wouldn't normally ask for help. I don't have to in my position. I'm a powerful man. People respect me. If anything, they're the ones who ask me to do things for them. I'm related to Herod Antipas, who rules Galilee for the Romans. I do some of his work in my part of the province. I have a big household. I'm used to telling people what to do. I don't have to ask for favours from anyone. But this time I had no choice. I either went and asked for help or watched my son die.

I told two of my slaves to saddle the horses and come with me to Cana, where this Jesus was staying. We soon found him, surrounded by a small group of his followers. I listened to his teaching for a few minutes. I could see straightaway that my status and my reputation would count for nothing with him. There would be no point making demands. So I got down on my knees and begged him to come back with me to Capernaum, while my son was still alive.

'You people only believe because you see signs,' he said. Well, maybe. I wasn't going to argue. It took a lot for a man like me to kneel before a man like him, a ruler pleading with a carpenter's son from Nazareth. I didn't tell him that, of course. I'm not sure I even thought it at the time. It may only have crossed my mind on the way home. This is what you do when all else fails and you're desperate. I just wanted him to come and heal my boy.

He wasn't what I expected of a healer. Yes, he listened to me telling him why I'd travelled over from Capernaum. But he refused point blank to come back with me. He told me to go home, that my boy would recover, that he'd live. He acted as if he was in charge of a situation he'd never even seen. Was he telling me I had to trust him if I wanted my boy to live, trust someone who's never even seen my son?

I'm not used to trusting people who won't do as I ask, however confidently they speak. But what he said was strong enough to send me and my two slaves back home. And when I arrived home I learnt that his words were stronger still.

How John uses the story of the royal official and his son

In the other Gospels, Jesus acquires much of his public reputation as a popular healer. In this Gospel there are only three healing stories, together with the raising of Lazarus from the dead. The healing of the royal official's son is the first of them, though there are earlier hints of this ministry in 2:23, 3:2 and 4:45. John locates Jesus' healing ministry among his seven signs. Yet both Jesus and John are cautious about them. When they are seen as pointing away from themselves, they reveal Jesus' glory (2:11). But when they are regarded as ends in themselves, the most they can do is to encourage the kind of response that Jesus is not prepared to trust (2:24; 6:26). They may make no impression at all (12:37), or even reinforce opposition to him from those who disputed the way he interpreted them as God's work (see 5:16-18, 36; 10:32, 33).

By taking Jesus back to 'Cana of Galilee where he had changed the water into wine', John turns the various episodes in chapters 2–4 into a single literary unit. Jesus is on a journey that takes him from Galilee to Jerusalem and back, via Judea and Samaria. He mixes with a wide range of people: members of his family, a village community, pilgrims in Jerusalem, traders in the temple, members of the ruling elites, John the Baptiser and his disciples in Judea, a Samaritan woman and people from her village, and now this high-ranking Jewish official. He moves between different geographical and social settings: Jewish and Samaritan villages, the Judean countryside, Jerusalem's temple and synagogue. He meets with a variety of responses, among them amazement, curiosity, welcome, questioning, bemusement, excitement and obedience. It is as if John is sketching out the world in which God's Sophia-Logos has pitched her tent, and the diversity of the new family into which those who receive him are born. Jesus' journey takes him across all kinds of geographical and cultural boundaries to show how the mission of God's love for the whole world opens up new possibilities for the whole human family.

With Jesus back in Cana, we can also see this healing having a 'third day' quality that turns it into an Easter event and anticipates the raising of Lazarus in chapter 11. One of the most important threads in that story is the absence of Jesus. He delays so long in responding to the sisters' message that Lazarus is dead by the time he arrives. Jesus' absence is a source of anxiety for John's audience, in view of the hostility they face from the synagogue. The healing of the official's son, like the raising of Lazarus from the dead, shows the power of Jesus' word despite his absence. His followers and friends should not equate distance and absence with indifference on his part. If the love he embodies crosses every kind of boundary, the word spoken from the beginning (1:1) invites trust across all time and space.

Reflections

Clive Marsh writes about the way the Gospels open us up to the presence of Christ outside the community of Jesus' disciples as well as within it.[32] The Gospels locate the life of Jesus within a number of 'patterns of living', among them inclusion, forgiveness, transformation and hospitality. Wherever we find these patterns embedded in what Marsh calls 'communities of practice' (family, friendship, church, work and education are the five he identifies), we can expect to discover Christ's hidden presence in our world.

Which 'patterns of living' and 'communities of practice' can you identify in the stories we have been reading from Jesus' journey between Cana, Jerusalem, Samaria and Cana again? Where can you see similar patterns and communities in your everyday world? How do John's stories help you to hear and respond to Christ's hidden presence there?

[handwritten notes:]
INCLUSION! — Ian Vander
    Children.
        Strange
Forgiveness — th'. My difficulty in
        letting go.
Transformation — I can't tell...
            others may.
Hospitality — Elspeth

---

32. Clive Marsh, *Christ in Practice. A Christology of Everyday Life*, London: Darton, Longman and Todd, 2006.

SEVEN

The paralysed man
John 5:1-18

Background

Jesus spends more time in Jerusalem in this Gospel than he does in the others. He is there for the Jewish festivals, though in this story we are not told which one it is. Having him in the city brings the controversy surrounding his ministry to the attention of the Jewish authorities early on, which turns his dispute with them into one of the main threads of the narrative. It is as if John has Jesus on trial throughout his ministry rather than at the end, before he is handed over to be crucified.

The pool of Bethzatha (some early copies of the Gospel have 'Bethesda') was in the north east of the city, just outside the city walls. It was originally built to supply water to the temple, though this function had been superseded in Jesus' day. By then it had acquired a reputation as a place of healing. Modern readers may feel that verse 4 – included as a footnote in many translations – smacks of superstition or magic. The professional physicians who were in the ascendant in Jesus' day would no doubt have thought the same. But this uncertain verse may underline the role of psychological factors in healing. Believing in the healing power of supposedly supernaturally disturbed water would certainly have contributed to any cure it brought. Bethzatha was still associated with healing a century after Jesus' visit. The Roman emperor Hadrian turned it into a healing shrine dedicated to the god Serapis after the second Jewish revolt in AD 135.

A healing pool on the edges of the city would make a natural gathering place for those who were sick and impaired. They were part of a larger company of poor and marginalised people, who supported themselves by begging and also included the most impoverished day labourers and prostitutes. They were turfed out of the city at nightfall, and spent the night in appalling conditions along the city walls and in hedgerows, before returning the next day. It has been estimated that they made up ten percent of Jerusalem's settled population. We can see something of the social isolation brought about by the paralysed man's condition in his remark in verse 7 that he had no one to take him to the pool when the water was disturbed.

To appreciate the significance of healing in Jesus' day, it is helpful to draw on the anthropological distinction between 'disease' as a bio-medical condition with a number of symptoms, and 'illness' as something that affects people socially as well as bodily. So in the case of leprosy, a range of skin conditions that included psoriasis, acne and a variety of rashes required sufferers to be isolated from the rest of the population to prevent further contamination. But leprosy was also regulated by the purity system, which was derived from the law of Moses (especially the Holiness Code of Leviticus 17–26) and divided everything into 'clean' and 'unclean' categories. Leprosy rendered sufferers 'unclean' because the boundary between an individual's body and the wider social body was deemed to be out of sorts. That made leprosy into an illness, not simply a disease. The healing of a leper required the skin to be restored and the person to be re-integrated into the community at the word of a priest who represented the purity system. This explains Jesus' practice of sending the lepers he healed to have their cure confirmed by a priest (interestingly, there are no instances of his healing lepers in this Gospel).

The purity system also regarded what we now call impairments as unclean. According to the purity laws in Leviticus 21:16-24, people who were blind or lame, or whose bodies were injured or malformed, were not allowed to worship at the altar. In the other Gospels, we are told that those who were thought to be possessed by spirits because their behaviour was unpredictable or uncontrollable were also labelled as 'unclean', and the stigma they carried only added to their distress. We can begin to imagine the isolation of the paralysed man and the community that gathered at the pool. Cut off from family and village and ostracised by the temple, they lived on the margins of life and hope.

The evangelists' accounts of Jesus' healings highlight the psychological and social dimensions of illness alongside the symptoms of disease. He drew out the faith of those who came to him for healing, and restored those he healed to their families and communities. He showed his concern for the whole person by offering not simply a cure for bodily symptoms, but a foretaste of God's all-embracing salvation. Occasionally he acknowledged some connection between sickness and sin, though without endorsing the popular understanding of misfortune as God's punishment. To label a group of people as 'sinners', as in 'tax collectors and sinners' in Luke 15:1, 2, was to make a social statement. Sinners were outcasts. Jesus seems to have shared the view that sickness was sinful in that it disrupted social relations. So when he told the man to 'go and sin no more so that nothing worse happens to you' in verse 14, he wanted him to make sure he avoided the worst possible form of social isolation in his day: having no one to remember him and bury him. /

Jesus' willingness to heal on the Sabbath is consistently controversial across all four Gospels. The command to observe the Sabbath in Exodus 20:8-11 was based on the interpretation of the creation story in Genesis 1, in which God is said to 'rest' on the seventh day after completing his work – though the version of the same commandment in Deuteronomy 5:12-15 sees the Sabbath rest as an opportunity to remember Israel's deliverance from Egypt rather than creation. Either way, the Sabbath gave a distinctive rhythm to Israel's life that helped to define their identity as God's covenant people. At a time when this was under pressure from the double occupation of Roman rule and foreign culture in their ancestral lands, keeping the Sabbath was a form of cultural resistance. Jesus defended his pressuring the boundaries of the purity system by reminding his critics that 'it is lawful to do good on the sabbath' (Matthew 12:12). Meeting human need provides the benchmark for that goodness and the key to interpreting the Sabbath laws. As Jesus said elsewhere, 'the sabbath was made for humankind, not humankind for the sabbath' (Mark 2:27).

Jesus' attitude to the Sabbath and the purity laws in general shows how the paralysed man and others like him were disempowered not only by their impairments but also by a system that condemned and excluded them. The authorities judged Jesus in the same way. Not only did his actions contradict their literal understanding of God's rest, they also raised serious questions about his fundamental loyalties. Jesus' critics naturally concluded that he could not possibly have been speaking on behalf of God, or behaving like a true son of God's covenant. Not unlike the way Mark ends an early series of conflict stories (see Mark 2:1–3:6), John shows Jesus aggravating their antipathy towards him, and provoking their determination to be rid of him.

I imagine the man at the centre of the story describing his life as a beggar in Jerusalem, and the way his condition had ostracised him from his family and village, until the power of Jesus' word restored his life.

The paralysed man's story

I don't know how I managed to get to the pool. I could hardly walk. I hadn't walked properly for 38 years. Not since the day I fell off the roof of our house as a boy. I shouldn't have been up there. My father was always telling me how dangerous it was to climb on the roof. To make matters even worse, it was the Sabbath. A rabbi saw me on his way back from the synagogue. 'What are you doing, climbing up there on the Sabbath? Don't you know you're breaking the law of Moses?' I was terrified. It felt like his words were so strong that they threw me off the roof. I landed on my back. I couldn't get up. I've never walked properly since – I can barely stand. I sinned on the Sabbath, the rabbi said. And this was my punishment.

Most of the men in my village worked on the land. I've never been able to work. I tried once or twice, but my legs just went from under me. I was a drain on my family. I lived with my sister and her family for a while after my parents died. But then it got too much for them. They couldn't provide for me as well as their children. I persuaded them to take me to Jerusalem. I knew I wouldn't be able to earn a living. I'd have to beg. But I'd get more from the city than my village. And no one knew me there.

My legs got worse, not better. I never did manage to get work. I lived rough, with others like me. We'd get thrown out of the city every night. We'd find shelter somewhere, anywhere, not too far away. Then we'd help each other to get back into the city the next morning. Down to the pool if we could. It was where we all gathered. Plenty of protection from the weather. Lots of visitors with money to spare passing by. I knew the people by the pool. Blind people. Paralysed people like me. People who'd fallen on hard times. We were poor. We lived by begging. We shared what we collected. We made sure we all had enough to eat. But we were a family of misfits and outcasts with nothing to look forward to.

One day a man came by the pool. I'd seen him before, but this was the first time he'd spoken to me. 'Do you want to be made well?' he asked. He looked me straight in the eye. Did he know the pool has healing powers? Some of the people here have friends who help them into the pool when the angel disturbs the waters. The first one in is healed. I thought that was what he meant. I could never get to the pool in time. I had no one to carry me into the water. Was he prepared to do that for me, this man I didn't know?

His next words startled me. 'Stand up.' I haven't stood up properly for 38 years, not since the day I fell off the roof. He looked me straight in the eye as he spoke to me. 'Stand up.' He didn't raise his voice. He wasn't angry with me. I could feel power in his words, even greater than the rabbi's words that flung me off the roof. I felt the energy of his words filling my whole body, like the breath of God filling Adam. The feeling began to return to my legs. They started to move. 'Stand up!' he said again, and I took hold of his hand. He pulled me to my feet. I felt unsteady. I hadn't stood unaided for so long. I took my first few steps with him, and then he disappeared in the crowd.

'Stand up, take your mat and walk.' His words were still ringing in my ears as I walked towards the temple carrying my mat. My legs were feeling stronger with every step. I wanted to thank God for what had happened to me. To pray and offer a sacrifice. I felt a bit unsteady, but my mind was full of the life I'd have once I could walk properly. I'd go back to my village and look for my family. I'd be able to work again. Then out of the blue I heard a loud voice behind me. 'What are you doing, carrying your mat on the Sabbath?' The voice of a rabbi, one of the Pharisees, coming from the synagogue, yelling at me. 'Don't you know you're breaking the law of Moses?' I'd forgotten what day it was.

His words nearly knocked me over, like the time I fell off the roof as a boy. But I knew I'd heard more powerful words that day, words that raised me to my feet. So I told the rabbi I was carrying my mat because I'd been healed. He wanted to know who'd done that to me on the Sabbath. It was then that I realised that I didn't know his name. But I found out who he was later, when I met him in the temple. So I went back to the synagogue to tell them that it was a man called Jesus from Nazareth who made me walk again. I felt sure they'd want to thank him, but not as much as I did.

How John uses the story of the paralysed man

This is the second of John's three healing stories, four if we include the raising of Lazarus in chapter 11. They are closely linked, and he clearly uses the relationships between them for dramatic effect. The uncontroversial healing of the royal official's son reveals the power of Jesus' word, which is strong enough to overcome death in the story of the raising of Lazarus in chapter 11. The healing of the man paralysed for 38 years also testifies to the power of Jesus' word, and anticipates the healing of the man who had been blind for the whole of his life in chapter 9. Both take place in Jerusalem on the Sabbath, and intensify the conflict between Jesus and the authorities. In the other Gospels, Jesus' healings highlight one of the characteristic themes of his ministry, his readiness to cross social boundaries, including those imposed by the purity system. But John is more interested in the way Jesus' healings provoke conflict with the authorities and trigger the processes that culminate in his crucifixion. Healings are signs of God's glory because the salvation they bring leads ultimately to the hour of Jesus' execution, when he is glorified (1:14; 12:23; 13:1; 17:1-5).

In the other Gospels, Jesus defends his sometimes controversial healing ministry by identifying what he does with the coming of God's kingdom or the Spirit promised by the prophets (Luke 4:16-20; 7:18-23; 11:19, 20), or with the activity of Sophia (Matthew 11:19, Luke 7:35). The Wisdom poems lie behind Jesus' reply to those who accuse him of breaking the Sabbath and making himself equal with God. As the narrative unfolds from verse 19 onwards, the scene shifts from the pool and the temple to the courtroom as Jesus begins his defence. In verses 19-24, he sees his healing work as fulfilling all that Sophia speaks of: the mutual love of God and Sophia, and God's unceasing work of creation through her. As the Son, Jesus loves the Father and is loved by him. He does what he sees his heavenly Father doing. This is what John means by Jesus' equality with God in 5:18. To see what Jesus does in restoring life to the lame man is to see what God is always doing by loving the world as he does. As Jesus will later tell Philip, 'whoever has seen me has seen the Father' (14:8-14). And there are even greater things to come, says Jesus in verses 25-29, as he looks ahead to raising Lazarus from death, and the day of judgement that this anticipates.

Jesus goes on in verses 30-46 to introduce an array of witnesses in his defence. First into the witness box is John the Baptist, whose testimony blazed the trail to Jesus, but no more. 'He was not the light, but came to testify to the true light' (1:8, 9). Then Jesus appeals to his own works, in particular the lame man's healing, which his opponents can only see as a breach of the Sabbath rather than a revelation of the life-giving presence and power of God. Next onto the stand is his heavenly Father, speaking presumably through Scripture, and especially in the evocative poetry of Sophia, which finds its fulfilment in Jesus. But the Father also confirms the work of Jesus through the Spirit that has remained on him ever since John the Baptist saw it descend from heaven like a dove (1:32). The healing of the impaired man is the creator Spirit revitalising the lifeless limbs of a man who has been lame for most of his life. Last into the witness box is Scripture, on which Jesus' enemies pin all their hopes and judgements. Yet they have no real affinity with the source of Scripture. 'You have never heard his voice or seen his form, and you do not have his word abiding in you.' Worse still, 'you do not have the love of God in you'. Instead they prefer the fractious, competitive world of human back-slapping and back-stabbing. With no desire for the honour that would puncture their own self-importance, there are no surprises in their rejection of God's emissary.

Does Jesus then pronounce judgement on them? There is no need. They are judged by the one whose teachings they claim to follow to the letter. 'If you believed Moses, you would believe me, for he wrote about me.' The trial continues in the exchanges that extend into the festival of Booths in chapter 7, when Jesus is next in Jerusalem. There too he teaches openly in the temple area, and appeals to Moses to condemn the authorities (7:19-24). His audiences debate among themselves whether Jesus is the messiah or the prophet promised by Moses. The temple police try to arrest him, and word gets back to the chief priests and Pharisees about the impact of his teaching. They are powerless to stop him, because 'his hour had not yet come' (7:30; 8:20). Yet the tension continues to mount, as Jesus speaks enigmatically of his imminent departure to a glorious place beyond their reach, from where the living waters of God's renewing Spirit will flow (7:33-39; 8:21-30). Jesus and the Jews both claim the authority of Abraham as well as Moses, but he accuses them of being children of the devil, and they accuse him of being a demonised Samaritan (8:39-59).

The narrative is clearly operating on two levels. On the earthly, public level we see typical power struggles within the family of Israel over who has the right to speak and act for God, with each trying to undermine the authority of the other. Here Jesus is vulnerable to popular opinion and political machination. John's audience knows the outcome of these struggles, and realises that in the end Jesus will become the inevitable victim of a system that relies on oppression and violence. But there is a heavenly, hidden level whose powers are at work to restrain Jesus' enemies without their knowing. Here Jesus is in control of his destiny. He knows who he is, where he has come from and where he is going, and how his death will bring God's blessing to the world. As John's story progresses, more sinister hidden powers emerge. The conflict between Jesus and his enemies in a tiny corner of the Roman empire, with its disputes over what should and should not happen on the Sabbath, reveals its true cosmic significance as an episode in the struggle between light and darkness.

Reflections

We have seen how John invites his audience to 'come and see' Jesus at home with different groups of insiders and outsiders. In Jerusalem once again, he is with another marginal community, the impaired and others who live on the edges of society. Jesus moves easily across the boundaries that identify and sometimes segregate different groups in his world, unfettered by the prejudices that obscure the humanity of the people he meets. Such free movement is a sign of the security his relationship with the one he calls 'Father' gives him. It also reveals his confidence that, in reaching out to whoever he meets, he is doing the work of God as the dwelling place of Sophia-Logos.

Words like 'insiders', 'outsiders', 'impaired' and 'disabled' reflect the vantage points of those who use them. Which individuals or groups do these words bring to mind from the worlds you move in and out of every day? How do you think they prefer to describe themselves?

Over the past 30 or so years, those who are on the receiving end of health and social care services have increasingly insisted that they should have their say in shaping the help they receive. 'Nothing about us without us' is the unifying demand of service-user movements intent on overcoming the disempowerment they have suffered as a result of ignorance, fear, prejudice and discrimination.[33] However well-meaning, traditional ways of providing services are now seen as patronising and insensitive when they bypass the real needs of those they seek to help in favour of the interests of service providers.

Healing stories like this one come from a world in which people who were marginalised because of illness or impairment had neither power nor hope. Unlike the members of today's service-user movements, those who gathered around the pool of Bethzatha were largely passive. The paralysed man could do nothing other than wait for someone to help him. If his story is to inspire today's readers, we may need to look hard for signs of empowerment in it. Where does Jesus enable him to play a part in his healing? How does this help you to read his story in an empowering way?

---

33. The website Shaping Our Lives provides a forum for members of service-user movements, in order to improve the quality of available support. See www.shapingourlives.org.uk

EIGHT

The hungry man in the large crowd
John 6:1-15

Background

The story of the feeding of a large crowd appears in all four Gospels. As we'd expect, there are common features. The people are drawn by Jesus' teaching and healing. The setting is somewhere near the Sea of Galilee (John also gives it its Roman name, the Sea of Tiberias, the Roman emperor at the time, to signal the foreign occupation of the Jewish ancestral lands). The amount of food at hand to feed a hungry crowd of at least 5000 people (John does not mention the number) is minuscule, and there is no possibility of buying food locally for so many. Yet Jesus takes what is available, the crowd are satisfied, and there is food to spare. Except in Luke, Jesus then becomes separated from his disciples, who cross the lake and a storm blows up. Jesus is eventually re-united with them by walking on the sea.

John has a number of distinctive elements. He has Jesus and his disciples on a mountain, like Moses and Elijah before them. The feeding takes place just before the Passover festival, which links it strongly with Jesus' execution. Jesus rather than the disciples asks how the crowd are to find food, though typically in this Gospel, he knows what he will do. The disciples discover that a lad in the crowd has loaves made from barley and a couple of fish. The leftovers are gathered up to avoid any waste. The crowds respond by acclaiming Jesus as the prophet expected by Moses in Deuteronomy 18:15-19, and they try to force him to lead them against the Romans.[34] He manages to escape, and this is what separates him from his disciples.

The abundance of food is a reminder of other stories in this Gospel: water into wine in chapter 2 and the large catch of fish in chapter 21. There are strong scriptural resonances with Jesus' feeding and his subsequent walking on the sea: the hungry people of Israel wandering through the wilderness, fed by Moses with manna from heaven; the prophets Elijah and Elisha feeding people who were hungry and poor

---

34. The Jewish historian Josephus (AD 37-100) tells of a number of prophets who were inspired by the story of Moses to lead popular liberation movements between AD 45 and 70. They led their followers into the desert, and expected to see signs of deliverance, including water from the rock and manna from heaven. These hopes were encouraged by the feasts of Passover and Tabernacles, which had strong connections with the memory of Moses. From what we know of popular expectations at the time, Moses' prophet was not the same figure as David's messiah, though John conflates them in verses 14 and 15.

in desperate circumstances;[35] and God's mastery of the threatening power of nature seen in floods and storms.

We should not allow the mysterious, even what we might call 'supernatural', elements of this account to obscure the mundane realities of Jesus' world. Then as now, food was subject to market forces, with supplies dependent on availability. The weather, harvests, transportation and politics played their part in determining food prices. The precariousness surrounding what is ultimately God's gift is certainly reflected in the sequel to the feeding in verse 26. Who could fail to be drawn to a man who seems to guarantee such easy, risk-free access to life's essentials?

In what follows, I let one of the crowd tell the story of the feeding.

The hungry man's story

It's nearly Passover. The festival really lifts our spirits. Passover is like walking through the sea with Moses and our ancestors. It makes us hungry for the land we were promised. Not that I can afford to go up to Jerusalem for the festival this year. Last year's harvest was worse than the year before. Money's tight. Food costs so much. I'm having to work extra hard to feed the family. I've finished for today, though. That's why I'm here with all these other people. Listening to this rabbi Jesus.

Did I say that Passover is the only way of keeping hope alive? That, and the rabbi Jesus. The stories he tells appeal to people like me. He talks in pictures. He speaks of things working men know about. He says that God's business is like running a vineyard or being a farmer or looking after sheep or fishing. I like his story about the world as a big wedding feast where everyone's invited and no one goes hungry. Even I can understand his kind of talk.

I wonder what the rabbis from the synagogue would make of a crowd like this. I've never seen so many people – except when Jerusalem is full at Passover. I recognise a lot of them. Farmers and fishermen. A group of Pharisees over there. Even a few women and children. And some soldiers. Are they expecting trouble? Or are they hungry for his teaching too?

Speaking of which, I'm famished. I didn't bring anything to eat. I wasn't expecting to be out so long. Or to be so far from home. There's no villages nearby where there might be spare food we could buy. Though they'd need a lot with this crowd. Has anybody brought anything to eat? I'm sure they'd share it if they had. No one goes hungry in our village – not if there's enough food to go round.

One of the rabbi's friends has found a young lad with some food. I can see from where I'm standing that there's not much. Barely enough

---

35. During a severe drought Elijah fed the widow of Zarapheth and her son with a handful of meal and a little oil in 1 Kings 17:8-12, and Elisha fed 100 people with a man's barley loaves in 2 Kings 4:42-44; only John mentions that Jesus fed a much larger number with barley loaves.

to feed the boy, let alone this lot. He's giving his food to Jesus. And now we're all being told to sit down. I'm glad about that. I've got a better view now. I'm near enough to see what the rabbi is doing with it. He's just looked up to heaven, and now he's giving the boy's food to his friends. They're bringing it round. How far do they expect a few loaves and fish to spread?

Now I can see other people starting to eat. And there's food for me too. And more on the way. And more still. 'No, thanks,' I say when the third lot comes round. 'I'm full, I've eaten enough.' We're all full. We've all had enough to eat. There's more than enough for everyone. It's like being at a feast or a festival. I wish we had this much food every day. We wouldn't have to worry about the price of grain and fish and oil then.

It's nearly Passover. The only way to keep hope alive, I would have said. Until now. Who is this rabbi Jesus? Is he another Moses, feeding hungry people out in the desert? Is he the prophet Moses wrote about? I'm not the only one who's asking. I'll go and talk to him, if I can get past all these people. I'll find out what he has to say for himself.

Hello, what's going on? I hope that's not trouble down there where Jesus was standing with his friends. The soldiers will be along before we know where we are. They don't stand any nonsense. I can't see Jesus now. Where's he gone? Has he been arrested? What kind of rabbi is he who can take our hunger away with just a few loaves and fishes?

How John uses the story of the feeding

Throughout this Gospel, Jesus' signs and associated words interpret each other. Water into abundant wine is a sign of Jesus' glory. Disturbing temple trade is a sign that a new centre of worship is coming. Healing a boy 20 miles away in Capernaum is a sign of the creative power of God's word. Restoring a chronically disabled man is a sign that God continues his ceaseless work of creation through Jesus. And now, feeding a large crowd with bread made from barley is a sign of the bread that nourishes a new dimension of life: eternal life, literally, 'life in the age to come'. Jesus draws God's future into the present, and feeds the life that it brings.

The feeding of the crowd is followed by an extended discourse that owes much to the rabbinic question-and-answer style of learning. It takes place in the synagogue in Capernaum, and is built around scriptures that may have been read at Passover-tide. Jesus' talk of eating heavenly bread and the life it brings makes repeated allusions to the poetry of Sophia, which he once again applies to himself. But what he says is largely lost on the crowds who have eaten their fill of barley bread and fish.

Jesus and his audience struggle to communicate. From the beginning, their conversation proceeds at two levels, the earthly and the heavenly, and as far as most of the crowd are concerned, the two never meet.

Once hungry and now satisfied with bread they did nothing to produce, they not surprisingly want more of the same. They cannot lift their horizons beyond the perishable bread of everyday life, which comes at a price that is governed by the laws of supply and demand. They remind us of Nicodemus, who could not see beyond natural birth, and the Samaritan woman, preoccupied at first with her daily duty of collecting water. Here as there, Jesus speaks metaphorically. 'Birth from above', 'living water' and now 'food that endures' are associated with the heavenly, eternal realm of 'spirit' not 'flesh' (verse 63). Does Jesus suggest that everyday concerns about birth, drink and food are less important than otherworldly, spiritual things? Or is he speaking of an alternative reality within the mundane world? This is entered through an experience that is birth-like, and is a dimension of life in which people are nourished with the wine and water that flow from him, and the bread that he gives.

Answers emerge as the dialogue proceeds. Jesus' audience want a sign of his authority to speak as he does about food that endures. At Passover-tide, they naturally have Moses and the signs he performed in mind. 'He gave them bread from heaven to eat' in verse 31 is the first of the Passover-tide scriptures. Exodus 16 tells the story of the manna in the wilderness and the water from the rock. But Jesus reminds the crowd that it was God, not Moses, who provided food and drink, before going on to speak of himself as 'the true bread from heaven (that) gives life to the world . . . the bread of life'.

'I am the bread of life' is the first of this Gospel's unique series of 'I am' sayings.[36] They draw on the revelation of the divine name to Moses in Exodus 3:14, and God's way of speaking through the prophet in Isaiah 43:3. Behind this opening saying lies Sophia's invitation to 'eat of my bread and drink of the wine I have mixed', and her offer of 'the bread of learning' and 'the water of wisdom'. The crowd's repeated misunderstanding and complaining, like the murmuring of their ancestors against Moses and God in the wilderness, serve John's purpose well by drawing out of Jesus what he means by his 'I am the bread of life'.

How can Jesus be 'the bread that came down from heaven' when everyone knows where he comes from, and who his parents are? What kind of bread has unlimited shelf life and nourishing power? What is this 'eating' that Jesus refers to when he speaks of heavenly bread as 'my flesh, given for the life of the world'? And how does it overcome death? The prophets are right[37] when they say that hungry people need divine help – and we might add, creative imagination – if they are to digest Jesus' metaphors.

---

36. The rest are 'I am the light of the world' (8:12), 'I am the gate for the sheep' (10:7), 'I am the good shepherd' (10:11), 'I am the resurrection and the life' (11:25), 'I am the way, the truth and the life' (14:6) and 'I am the true vine' (15:1). All these sayings are illuminated by the poetry of Wisdom: Jesus speaks as the dwelling place of Sophia-Logos.
37. John 6:45 draws on Isaiah 54:13 and Jeremiah 31:34.

In the Wisdom poetry, eating and drinking are metaphors of the faith that welcomes Sophia's divine teaching and lives wisely with the grain of God's good creation. For John this takes a particular form, expressed in verse 56: 'those who eat my flesh and drink my blood abide in me, and I in them'. Jesus' words about eating the bread of life point forward to the parable of the true vine in chapter 15, where fruitful life is only possible by mutual abiding: 'abide in me as I abide in you'. This means 'keeping my commandments [and] abiding in my love, just as I have kept my Father's commandments and abide in his love'. Love like this is modelled by Jesus' 'greater love . . . to lay down one's life for one's friends'. When Jesus is no longer physically present, his love is embodied in the community that lives by his 'new commandment, that you love one another, just as I have loved you' (13:34, 35).

Sacrificial, Christ-like mutual love is the life that grows from the inner nourishment provided by the bread of life, which is 'my flesh, for the life of the world'. The community that abides in this love is hope-filled: 'those who eat my flesh and drink my blood have eternal life, and I will raise them up on the last day'. Even now, they experience something of the victory of Jesus' 'greater love' over every kind of death, as the dramatic raising of Lazarus in chapter 11 will reveal.

Eating Jesus' flesh and drinking his blood have strong eucharistic overtones. John replaces the account of Jesus' instituting the Lord's Supper on the night that he was betrayed with his washing the disciples' feet, another symbol of his self-sacrificing love (13:1-20). John is more interested in eucharistic living than eucharistic liturgy. This is the message of the bread of life discourse. Eating and drinking the gifts of Jesus-Sophia means believing and abiding, which nourish a community in faithfulness and loyalty to Jesus and one another. John's audience lives out this two-fold solidarity in the face of hostility from 'the world' (15:18–16:4). As the human face of Jesus, they stand in the same relation to God and the world as he does. 'Remember the word that I said to you, "Servants are not greater than their master." If they persecuted me, they will persecute you.' Eucharistic living shows itself in costly love. It is the privilege and the price of solidarity with brothers and sisters who are victimised for their loyalty to Jesus.

This is too much for Jesus' audience in the synagogue. Some of his disciples there find his words about consuming his flesh and blood so disturbing that they withdraw from his company (6:60-66). Their counterparts in John's audience are the secret disciples who wear their loyalty to Jesus lightly when the local synagogue threatens to exclude them, like those whom Jesus addresses in his conversation with Nicodemus. They fail to see how Sophia's bread can have anything to do with self-sacrificing love. What Jesus means will become clearer after his exaltation, when 'the Son of Man has ascended to where he was before'. For now he insists that he speaks with God's authority: his words are 'spirit and life', just as God is spirit and the ceaseless giver of life that defies death (4:24; 5:21).

Only the twelve remain. This is the first time John mentions them as a group. Peter's declaration of loyalty reminds us of his confession at Caesarea Philippi in the other Gospels (Mark 8:29 and parallels), though it is more muted here, to leave room for Martha's full-blown response to Jesus' 'I am the resurrection and the life' in 11:27. Here it is Judas, not Peter as in Mark's Gospel, whom Jesus calls a devil, anticipating the dark tones of John's later portrait of him. Judas is the antithesis of loyalty and solidarity, breaking bread with Jesus and the others but also breaking fellowship and trust. In John's eyes, nothing can be more worthy of God's judgement.

Reflections

Jesus' words in the synagogue after the feeding of the crowd distinguish the literal and symbolic interpretation of his capacity to nourish, yet without allowing the 'spirit' of his words to become spiritualised. He insists that eucharistic feeding makes a real difference in the world, not least to the care of his brothers and sisters who have a lot to lose because of their loyalty to him.

By contrast, the Episcopal Church of St Gregory of Nyssa in San Francisco holds together the literal and symbolic meaning of eucharistic bread in its Friday food pantry ministry, in which food is distributed to 800 families each week. The inspiration came from the journalist Sara Miles, who as a dedicated atheist walked in off the street in 1999, received the bread and wine and was converted there and then. In her words, 'the mysterious sacrament turned out to be not a symbolic wafer but actual food – indeed, the bread of life'. At St Gregory's and a number of other churches inspired by its witness, eucharistic worship shapes social outreach because the church does not distinguish between being spiritually fed and literally fed.[38]

Many churches define the authenticity of the Eucharist in terms of authorised presidency or reception of the sacrament. St Gregory's has an alternative vision that is rooted in the example and teaching of Jesus. How might these alternative visions of eucharistic living inspire you and your church to avoid spiritualising the 'spirit' of Jesus' words about the bread of life?

---

38. Sara Miles writes about her experience in *Take This Bread. The spiritual memoir of a twenty-first century Christian*, Norwich: Canterbury Press, 2012.

NINE

The woman brought before Jesus
John 7:53–8:8

Background

This story is only found in John's Gospel. Footnotes in our Bibles indicate that the earliest manuscripts of the Gospel didn't include it. Those that did placed it after 7:36, or at the end of chapter 21, which itself reads like a later addition. Some manuscripts included it in Luke's Gospel, after 21:38, when Jesus was in Jerusalem for Passover, just as the plots to have him put to death were taking shape. These various locations make it look like a story in search of a home. It does not fit the flow of John's Gospel at the end of chapter 7. Jesus' controversial encounters with the authorities usually provoke further discussion, as we have seen in the last three chapters. But there is none of that here. The woman appears, then disappears. Her story does not seem to connect with any of John's major themes.

The synoptic Gospels appear to offer a more fitting setting. Jesus' probing beyond the letter of the law of Moses to what goes on behind the scenes in human hearts and minds reflects the teaching of those parts of the Sermon on the Mount in which Jesus calls for a more radical approach to keeping the law of Moses (Matthew 5:21-47). There is a further connection with the synoptic Gospels in the account in Luke 7:36-38 of the woman who washes Jesus' feet with her tears and dries them with her hair, before kissing them and anointing them with ointment from an alabaster jar. Luke leads us to believe that she has received forgiveness through Jesus. The fact that she is a prostitute makes me wonder whether the same is true of the woman in this story. I assume that she is in the way I imagine her telling her story.

However much her story belongs with the world of the synoptic Gospels, it is not entirely out of place in John. The woman's social status reminds us of other characters in this Gospel. The Samaritan woman in chapter 4 was doubly marginalised in Jewish eyes, on the grounds of her race and gender, and a likely target for sexual stigmatisation from her own community on account of her irregular lifestyle. The paralysed man in chapter 5 and the man born blind in chapter 9 were economically poor, and regarded as social outcasts on account of their disabilities. The relationship between the law of Moses and the authority of Jesus runs throughout John's account of Jesus' public ministry in Jerusalem. A woman caught in the act of adultery provides a suitable test-case for a rabbi who is known to sit loose to some aspects of the law, particularly where it has a bearing on social inclusion. Jesus' refusal to judge her illustrates his statement to the authorities in 8:15: 'I judge no one.' And his final words to her, 'Do not sin again', echo what he said to the paralysed man in 5:14.

The laws on stoning as the punishment for adultery in Leviticus 20:10 and Deuteronomy 22:22 applied to both parties. According to Deuteronomy 13:9 and 17:7, those who witnessed capital offences were expected to initiate the stoning, followed by other members of the community. Under the Roman occupation, Jews did not have the right to execute anyone, though John records frequent attempts to stone Jesus, and in Acts 7:54–8:1, Luke tells of the stoning of Stephen, the first martyr from the Jesus movement. By bringing the woman before him, Jesus' opponents test not only how he sees his authority in relation to Moses, but also to Rome. A clear and unambiguous answer would land Jesus in trouble, either with Jewish law or Roman rule. Jesus' ability to turn the tables on his enemies is found in other accounts of his testing, notably in the synoptic accounts of his final days in Jerusalem (see Mark 11:27–12:37).

One of the most puzzling features of this story is Jesus' bending down to write on the ground with his finger. We have no idea what he wrote, or why he did it. Explanations range from embarrassment on his part (hardly likely in view of the disreputable company he keeps) to giving himself time to consider his response. His actions certainly heighten the dramatic tension in the story, as the woman's accusers become more insistent on provoking a reaction from him.

I imagine the woman recalling the way she has been used by men, and the very different interest that Jesus takes in her – something that she is not used to.

The woman's story

Do you think I enjoy selling my body for a living? Do I look forward to lying with the kind of man who'll pay for the pleasure of my company? They use me when it suits them, then throw me away when they've finished. Until next time. Soldiers. Builders. Merchants. Even pilgrims. Men away from home, in a place where nobody knows them. I don't ask too many questions. I just give them what they want, and hope to heaven they don't rough me up.

How long do you think I've been doing this? Prepare to be shocked. Since I was a child. It started at home. It all seemed very innocent at first. My mother turned a blind eye. Then my father started renting me out to his friends. You can imagine the rest. I've never known anything else for as long as I can remember. I moved from my village to the city after my father and mother died. I was hoping to put my past behind me. But what was I supposed to do with my life? How else could I make a living? This is all I've ever known.

The authorities wish I wasn't here – though they're not all they seem, but we won't go into that just now. They'd prefer it if my kind didn't exist. At least that's the impression they like to give. They won't admit it, of course, but I think they see what we do as unavoidable, even essential. Do you think that if we weren't here, men wouldn't want what we offer? We get regular warnings: 'clean up, or we'll clear you out'. But they're never more than threats. They never amount to much.

Except for the last time they picked on me. It was a set-up. The man I was with wasn't my usual kind. They weren't interested in him, of course. It was me they wanted. But why then? What was so special about that particular day? It turned out that it wasn't me they wanted to punish. They were just using me – what's new? – to get one over on someone else.

They barged into my room, dragged me off to the temple and threw me at the feet of a rabbi who was teaching in one of the courtyards. He'd drawn a big crowd. All men. 'We caught her with a man,' they shouted to the rabbi. 'You can see what kind of woman she is. Moses wrote that people like her should be stoned. What do you say we should do with her?'

They were no better than the other men who take my body. They had no more respect for me. They were using me. Rabbis arguing with each other. Men fighting men. I was just a plaything in their hands. I know that when they'd finished with me, they'd disappear like the rest. Until next time – if I survived, that is.

The noise. The shouting. 'What do you say about her, Jesus of Nazareth? What should her punishment be?' Even if he'd answered, I doubt they would have heard what he said above the crowd. 'Stone her, stone her, stone her!' All I could see was feet. People on their feet, shouting for blood. And his feet.

And then his hand and his finger. He bent down next to me and wrote something in the dust. The shouting got louder and louder. 'What do you say we should do with her?' 'Stone her, stone her, stone her!' Then, as suddenly as they'd barged into my room, it all went very quiet. The rabbi was on his feet. Everyone could hear what he said. I'll never forget his words. 'If there's anyone here who's never sinned, come and throw the first stone.'

All I could see was feet. People on their feet all around me. Not a sound, no one moved. Except him, as he bent down again and wrote something else in the dust. And then I saw them start to move away. The crowds who'd been listening to his teaching. The men who'd thrown me at his feet. I heard the sound of their footsteps. The breeze blew the dust they made into my face. But no shouting now, just a low murmur.

By the time I had the courage to stand up, it was just the rabbi and me. I'd never been in the temple before. I'm not even sure I should have been where I was. But that didn't bother him. 'There's no sign of your accusers,' he said. 'And I'm not going to condemn you.' His only interest in my body was when he told me to clean up my life.

Easier said than done. How will I get over my years of shame? What do I have to do to get rid of a reputation like mine? How does a woman like me start to earn an honest living?

He's the first man to show me any respect. It's a start.

How the woman's story fits into John's Gospel

Though this story was not originally part of John's Gospel, we have seen that it does reflect some of his themes and concerns. One of these is his use of John the Baptiser's witness to Jesus as 'the Lamb of God who takes away the sin of the world' in 1:29. The evangelist links this with his account of Jesus' passion by having Jesus condemned before Pilate at about noon on the day of Preparation for the Passover, as the lambs are being slaughtered (19:14). As far as we know, the Passover lamb was not seen as a sin offering at the time of Jesus. But this is how John seems to understand it. Some Jewish texts use 'Lamb of God' as a title for the messiah. John may be saying that Jesus is only ever Israel's freedom-bringing messiah as the one who sacrifices his life for the world, and thereby liberates people from their sins. According to John 19:30, Jesus dies with the triumphant announcement that his work is finished. But his ability to overcome sin is seen throughout his ministry, not only at the end, as the story of his encounter with the woman shows.

This Gospel reveals something of the complexity of sin. At one level sin is unbelief, the refusal to recognise God as the giver of life and Jesus as his emissary. What we might call the spiritual dimension of sin (because unbelief is the refusal to embrace God as life-giving Spirit) is overcome by Jesus absorbing his enemies' rejection of him, rather than recycling the violence they inflict. Their rejection culminates in his crucifixion, but the outcome of his passion and exaltation overturns the unbelieving world's verdict on him. The coming of the Spirit as God's advocate vindicates Jesus before those who judge him to be the agent of sin (16:8-11).

Sin is also a social condition, as we saw in the case of the paralysed man. On this understanding, sin ruptures relationships between individuals and social groups. Jesus demonstrates his determination to overcome this dimension of sin by showing solidarity with marginalised people and groups, such as the disabled, Samaritans and women. The unnamed adulterous woman belongs with the other women in John's Gospel who bear witness to Jesus' power over both the spiritual and social dimensions of sin.

John shows how Jesus the Lamb of God takes away the sin of the world, through the risks he takes in his ministry and the ultimate victory of his passion, exaltation and sending of the Spirit. The evangelist understands the victory and vindication of Jesus as his call to his followers to share in his work of freeing the world from the destructive power of sin in all its complexity. John records the risen Christ saying: 'Peace be with you. As the Father has sent me, so I send you ... Receive the Holy Spirit. If you forgive the sins of any, they are forgiven them; if you retain the sins of any, they are retained' (20:21-23). Jesus' response to the woman caught in the act of adultery – like his later conversation with Peter by the lakeside in chapter 21 – is an object lesson in the practice of forgiveness that lies at the heart of his disciples' vocation.

Reflections

Forgiveness is so central to the Christian Gospel that it is sometimes easy to underestimate the cost of forgiving. Some Christians suffer the most unimaginable atrocities and find themselves able to forgive immediately. This has a profound impact on the wider community, including those who have violated them. But other Christians find forgiveness difficult, if not impossible, despite the encouragement and example of Jesus. When we find it difficult to forgive, it can be helpful to realise that forgiveness is more of a journey than an event. It can take time to forgive when we have to process the hurt we've endured, and simply forgiving is not an option.

Jesus' bending down to write on the ground before standing to deliver his verdict is a sign that he took his time to respond to the woman and those who were calling for her to be stoned. The Lamb of God takes away the sins of the world by embracing and absorbing the experiences and emotions associated with sin, in its spiritual and social dimensions. Calvary is not simply an event, but the climax of the journey that constitutes his ministry as a whole.

Where have you come across people for whom forgiveness was less like a one-off event and more of a costly process?

Jesus' response to the woman and the baying crowd of men has been likened to the process of conflict resolution.[39] His initial response to her appearance before him de-escalates the situation, and reduces the risk of violence against the woman by lowering the level of emotional arousal in the crowd. His bending down to write on the ground is a piece of intriguing body language that draws attention away from the woman to himself. When he eventually speaks, he diverts attention away from himself and the woman towards those who have brought her, and places responsibility for the outcome in their hands not his. We can imagine Jesus' movement in all this as descent and ascent, a reflection of the incarnation and exaltation of Sophia-Logos, which is John's image of the way God's grace comes to redeem the world.

Where have you seen attempts to resolve conflict that mirror Jesus' movement of grace?

---

39. I am grateful to the Revd Ruth Adams, Vicar of St George's, Chesterton, Cambridge and the Bishop of Ely's Advisor for Resilience in Conflict, for introducing me to this.

TEN

The man born blind
John 9:1-41

Background

John's accounts of the healing of two men – one paralysed, the other born blind – have a lot in common. Both healings take place in Jerusalem on the Sabbath, and provoke controversy. Each involves a pool. In both cases Jesus takes the initiative in healing, and looks for both men later in the story. Both stories reflect popular beliefs about the connections between sickness and sin. The disciples assume that the blind man's misfortune is God's punishment for individual or family wrongdoing. Jesus reckons otherwise. He sees sickness as an opportunity to do God's work and reveal God's glory by acting compassionately, and makes much the same point when he hears about Lazarus' illness in 11:4.

For all their similarities, the stories have their differences. In the first, Jesus bears the brunt of the authorities' wrath, and the ensuing exchanges make it look as if they are putting him on trial. In the second, Jesus and the Pharisees never meet. Instead they interrogate the man and his family as if they are witnesses in Jesus' trial. But the more pressure they put on the man, the more determined he becomes to show his loyalty to Jesus. This is where the main difference between the two stories lies. John makes little of the paralysed man's faith, but his account of the healing of the blind man treats his developing faith in Jesus as one of its leading themes.

By using sight as a metaphor for faith, John echoes Mark's intriguing story of the two-stage healing of the blind man at Bethsaida (Mark 8:22-26). This is sandwiched between a particularly frustrating conversation between Jesus and his disciples about their lack of insight, and Peter's confession of faith in Jesus as the messiah at Caesarea Philippi. Mark seems to be saying that, despite their spiritual blindness, the disciples can come to recognise him for who he is, though not easily. Mark later tells the story of the healing of Bartimaeus as Jesus and his company pass through Jericho, on the way to Jerusalem for the final Passover (Mark 10:46-52). Between Caesarea Philippi and Jericho, Jesus has been talking about the way he will be received in Jerusalem. He expects to be rejected and killed, which only adds to the disciples' confusion and distress. They find it difficult to 'see' what he means. Then Bartimaeus the blind beggar overcomes the attempts of the surrounding crowd to silence him. He manages to attract Jesus' attention, and declares enough faith in him to receive his sight. The story ends with the now-seeing Bartimaeus following Jesus as a disciple on the way to the cross.

Like Bartimaeus, John's man born blind struggles against the odds to find his way to faith. We know nothing of the price Bartimaeus paid to become a follower of Jesus, but John leaves us in no doubt about the cost of discipleship for the man in his story, and others who believe in Jesus as he does.

I imagine the man born blind looking back to his meeting with Jesus, and how it changed his experience of trust.

The blind man's story

I wasn't the only blind person in my family. My parents told me that my grandfather and my uncle both went blind in their thirties. I'd never been able to see. I was born blind. Why did God punish our family like this? What had we done to deserve this curse? We never stopped asking the questions, but we never found an answer that made sense to us.

When you're blind you don't know for certain what life is like beyond your own body. I couldn't even tell the difference between day and night. I had to learn a different way of seeing. I developed another kind of sight. I relied on other people's eyes. I trusted whatever they told me. 'Over here.' 'Not that way.' 'It's safe to cross the street.' I saw with my other senses. I knew when it was daybreak because I heard the dawn chorus. I could smell the market place and taste the temple. I recognised people by the way they spoke. A touch was as good as a smile or a scowl. Because I'd lived in the same house with my parents all my life, I built up a picture in my mind of my surroundings.

Trust was my vision. The only way I could see.

I couldn't earn my own living. No farmer will hire a man who can't see where the seed falls or which olives are ready for picking. No trader will let a blind man sell his goods in the marketplace. My parents were too poor to feed me. So from an early age I begged. The city is full of beggars. But it's even more full of visitors and pilgrims. I lived off kindness and pity. Begging was a risky business. There are always those who take advantage of blind beggars, and steal what others have given.

Trust was my vision. Sometimes it let me down.

It was when I was begging one day in the city that I met a stranger. I didn't recognise his voice. I could tell by the way he spoke that he wasn't from these parts. I guessed he was from Galilee. I heard someone ask him whose fault it was that I couldn't see. I'd lived with that question for so long that I'd given up trying to find the answer. My parents always followed Moses' teachings. And their parents before them. They were no more sinful than anyone else. 'Whose sin blinded him?' The stranger didn't seem interested in the question. He was more concerned to do something about it.

He said his name was Jesus, and that he would help me to see. He told me how he would do it. He made a paste with dust and spit. He spread it over my eyelids. Then he said that I had to do something: 'wash yourself in the pool of Siloam'. I had no idea where that was. Someone led me there by the hand and helped me to take off my cloak, and then he went into the pool with me and held me while I washed myself.

Trust was my vision. Without it, Jesus' help would come to nothing.

The mud paste had dried by the time I reached the pool. As I stepped in I could feel it coming off. It was like drawing back a curtain and letting light into a room. Or in my case, letting light into my whole body for the first time ever. I knew something was happening to my eyes. Not that I could see clearly at first. That took a while. I could see something rather than nothing. Light rather than darkness. Vague shapes started to appear. The man helped me out of the pool, and took me back to my home. //

Over the next few days my sight improved. I saw faces for the first time. I found my way round the house without stretching out my hands. I walked into the city by myself, to the place where I used to beg. People were amazed that I could now see. But they weren't all as happy as I was. They kept asking, 'is he really the man who used to beg here?' Some said I was, others weren't convinced. What annoyed me was that they spoke as if I wasn't there. I had to keep saying, 'Yes, it's me. I was the blind beggar who sat there every day for as long as I can remember. But now I can see.'

Trust was still my vision, even with my eyes. But why didn't they trust me?

I told them about Jesus, and how he filled my whole life with light. Some Pharisees from the synagogue were even less happy than the people who didn't believe I'd been healed. They wanted to know every detail of what had happened to me. I felt like a criminal on trial. I told them my story, but they said they didn't trust Jesus. It was the Sabbath when he healed me, so that meant he couldn't possibly be from God. He must be a sinner. Or perhaps I wasn't really blind, and we were both deceivers. So they went and asked my parents. 'Yes, he was born blind,' they said. What else could they say? They were afraid of the Pharisees, too scared to mention Jesus. They said I was old enough to speak for myself. So I was dragged before the Pharisees a second time. They wanted me to agree with them that Jesus was a sinner. How could I say that? I didn't even know him. I met him once, very briefly, less than a week ago. I told them what happened to me again. 'In my eyes, he must be a prophet,' I said. 'He can't be a sinner, he must be from God. Don't we believe that God said "Let there be light"? Because of this man Jesus, my whole body is full of light. As far as I'm concerned, he really is from God.'

Trust may have been my vision, but it certainly wasn't theirs. In my eyes they were as good as blind.

They accused me of insulting them, and Moses too. They told me to stay away from the synagogue. They didn't want me stirring up trouble. Is it such a great loss, to have to stay away? I never really felt

I belonged there on account of my blindness. Jesus was still around in the city when he heard the news. He came and spoke with me. He asked me if I believed that God had sent him. I told him how much I trusted him, now that my own life could tell the story of God's light coming into a dark world. I'm sure I'll find my true home now with the people who believe in him. There are quite a few in the city.

What have I learnt from all this? A lot about trust. No matter how good my eyes are now, trust is still my vision. It's how I've come to see Jesus. But I know that trust is not everyone's vision.

How John uses the story of the blind man

Since 7:10, Jesus has been at the week-long festival of Booths (its Hebrew name 'Succoth' is also translated 'Tabernacles'). This autumn event was one of the three great festivals of the Jewish year (the others were Passover and Pentecost), and was named after the makeshift huts in which the Hebrews lived during their journey through the wilderness with Moses (Leviticus 23:33-44). Booths was originally a harvest festival, and prayers for winter rain and the renewal of sunlight were offered. Its daily ceremonies included a procession from the fountain of Gihon on the south east side of the temple hill, which supplied water to the pool of Siloam. Here a priest filled a golden pitcher with water and the temple choir sang the words of Isaiah 12:3: 'With joy you will draw water from the wells of salvation.' The procession entered the temple through the Water Gate, accompanied by psalm-singing pilgrims carrying bunches of myrtle and willow twigs to symbolise their ancestors' wilderness dwellings. The ceremony reached its climax when the priest poured out the water by the altar of burnt offerings in front of the temple. On the last day of the feast, the priest circled the altar seven times before he poured out the water. It was at this moment that Jesus issued Sophia's invitation to the thirsty to 'come to me and drink' (7:37, 38).

Jesus' 'I am the light of the world' belongs with another of the festival's ceremonies that celebrated the journey through the wilderness. According to Exodus 13:17-22, God led Moses and the people in a pillar of cloud during the day and a pillar of fire by night. On the first night of Booths, four golden candlesticks are lit in an area of the temple called the Court of Women, through which the water procession passed every day. As the temple is flooded with light, Jesus once again speaks as Sophia, 'a reflection of eternal light, a spotless mirror of the working of God' (Wisdom 7:26). His words span the beginnings of Genesis and the Gospel of John, as they do when he smears mud paste on the eyes of a man who has never before seen the light. Life and light enter where previously death and darkness reigned. So the evangelist turns the healing of the blind man into a parable of God's ceaseless creativity, yet another sign of Jesus doing the work of God as Sophia-Logos made flesh.

Light and darkness characterise John's dualistic, either/or world. It has no grey areas. 'Whoever follows me will never walk in darkness, but will have the light of life' (8:12). Jesus has already challenged Nicodemus and those like him from the synagogue to come out of the shadows into the bold light of baptism, with its public confession of faith in Jesus. John uses the healing of the man born blind to intensify that earlier appeal. He experiences a kind of baptism by immersing himself in a pool named like Jesus, Siloam/Sent. He emerges as if born from above, of water and the Spirit, as light floods his whole body for the first time. And, most importantly, he has the courage to stand his ground before those who seek to undermine his integrity.

John's world may be black and white, but his Gospel is a vivid tapestry of symbols and metaphors, nowhere more so than in this story. Jesus' words can be drained of all their colour by interpreting them literally. This is what Nicodemus, the Samaritan woman and the Jews in Capernaum do when Jesus speaks of being 'born from above', the gift of 'living water', and the possibility of 'eating my flesh and drinking my blood'. The Pharisees too, at the end of this story, fail to get beyond the literal meaning of blindness and seeing (9:40, 41). But as the man's story unfolds, the evangelist weaves it into a parable of the metaphorical sense of sight – seeing as insight into the identity of Jesus, sight as faith in Jesus as the one sent by God.[40] Like Naaman the Syrian leper, who came to believe in the authority of Israel's God by obeying the prophet Elisha's command to wash in the river Jordan (see 2 Kings 5:10-14), the blind man obeys Jesus' command to wash and his eyes are gradually opened to the world's true light.

Soon after he has received his sight, he tells those who have only known him as a blind beggar what 'the man called Jesus' did for him. When the Pharisees investigate a healing they find offensive because it contravenes the Sabbath regulations, the man sides with those who reject their conclusion that Jesus must be a sinner, and declares that 'he is a prophet'. His defiance provokes the Pharisees (or 'the Jews' as they are called in the rest of the narrative), and they set out to discredit his testimony. First they call on his parents to verify that the man is their son and that he was indeed born blind. Though they are willing to confirm his identity, they are too frightened to say why he can now see: 'ask him; he is old enough to speak for himself'. So for the second time the authorities grill their son, who again refuses to accept that Jesus is a sinner. He is astonished at his interrogators' ignorance over Jesus' origins. Surely they must realise that one who

---

40. David Hyerle maps the everyday uses of the 'seeing' metaphor in his *Visual Tools for Transforming Information into Knowledge*, Thousand Oaks, California: Corwin Press, 2009 (2nd edition), p. 19. We speak of seeing as knowing, reflection as self-knowing, visual acuity as clear thinking, getting situations into perspective, being focused, having tunnel vision, blind spots, oversight, visionary people, and so on. The healing of the man born blind is an invitation to incorporate the richness of this metaphor into the practice of faith.

does something so unprecedented and creative must be 'from God'. This proves too much for the Jews, who insult him before expelling him from the synagogue. But their hostility serves only to increase his vision. At the climax of the story when he meets Jesus again, he makes the full Johannine confession of faith in Jesus the Son of Man, and in anticipation of Thomas at the end of the Gospel, worships him as Lord.

The man's faith grows in the face of hostility on the part of the Jewish authorities, who seem to be engaged in an official enquiry, almost a trial. In their eyes the man is not worthy to remain in the synagogue community. His courageous faith contrasts sharply with those whom the evangelist criticises in 12:42-44, at the end of Jesus' public ministry. In his earlier exchange with Nicodemus, Jesus challenged people like them to have the courage to be baptised. Some of the synagogue's secret sympathisers are of high standing in their community, and the loss of reputation is too much to pay for loyalty to Jesus. John may well see the man born blind as a role model for those in his audience who are threatened with expulsion from the synagogue, and even death, because of their faith in Jesus (9:22, 12:42, 16:2). This is more likely to reflect a localised breakdown of relationships between the synagogue and Christ-followers rather than something more widespread. But the emerging (in)sight of the man born blind has a wider appeal to all whose loyalty to Jesus is tested by instances of what John sees as the world's darkness. Once again the evangelist uses the testimony of an outcast, whose faith bears witness to the light that shines in the darkness without being overcome by it (1:5).

Reflections

The connections John makes between believing and seeing in this story are a reminder that this is a visual Gospel. Its rich symbolism appeals to the imagination of those whose lives are shaped by visual rather than verbal culture. John reminds us that however important reasoning might be – and his Gospel certainly gives us a lot to think about – symbols are powerful ways of communicating the story of Jesus. Yet if faith is a kind of 'seeing' (and this goes back to Jesus' first words in the Gospel at 1:39: 'come and see'), this is more than aesthetic experience, as David Hyerle's mapping of the metaphor suggests. John Hick writes of faith as 'experiencing as', that is, responding wholeheartedly to the world as mediating the activity and call of God. In Christianity, what is 'seen' in the person of Jesus Christ acts as the catalyst for this way of faith.[41]

---

41. John Hick, *Faith and Knowledge*, Glasgow: Collins Fontana Books, 1974, especially chapters 5, 6 and 9.

This suggests that David Csinos' symbol- and action-centred approaches to spiritual experience belong together.[42] This is certainly the case in John 9. The blind man 'sees' and then resists every attempt to undermine him. In your reading of John's Gospel, what do you 'see' in Jesus? How does this shape the way you respond to him in your life as a whole?

There is a flip-side to the positive message of this story. If sight is associated with light and faith, blindness is equated with their opposites. To use a physical impairment as a metaphor for unbelief and hostility is as unacceptable today as the negative stereotyping endemic in racism, sexism and many other forms of prejudice. The theologian John Hull, who died in 2015, lost his sight in 1980 at the age of 45. This led him to view the Bible as the product of a sighted culture with a negative attitude towards blindness. By contrast, he adopted a positive attitude to impairment, despite his experience of what he called 'deep blindness', a state in which he had lost all his visual memory, imagery and orientation. He argued that people with impairments can help the Church to be itself, first by drawing attention to the way societies turn impairments into disabilities, and then by encouraging the Church to welcome those who appear to be different. He believed that, as a community of inclusive love, the Church rediscovers its prophetic calling to be a symbol of the kingdom of God.[43]

What kind of welcome does your church or neighbourhood or workplace give to people with impairments? How do you pray with and for those whom society considers to be 'disabled'?

Or impoverished
Homeless.
LGBT.
Failed.
Psychologically ill

---

42. See above, page 26, in the chapter on John the Baptiser.
43. John Hull's story of his journey into blindness is told in his *Touching the Rock*, London: SPCK 2016, 2nd edition, and in the film by Peter Middleton and James Spinney, *Notes on Blindness* (2016). Hull contributed a theological understanding of disability to *Disability. An Inclusive Church Resource*, London: Darton, Longman and Todd, 2014. For a more comprehensive coverage see Brian Brock and John Swinton (eds.), *Disability in the Christian Tradition. A Reader*, Grand Rapids/Cambridge: Eerdmans, 2012.

ELEVEN

Mary, the sister of Lazarus
John 11:1–12:7

Background

Lazarus, Martha and Mary appear from nowhere in this Gospel. Unlike many of the other characters Jesus meets, we know their names and where they live, but that is all. We do not know who they are, or where their obviously close relationship with Jesus comes from. Luke 10:38-42 tells of two sisters, Martha and Mary, who offer hospitality to Jesus and his disciples. But there is no mention of a brother, or where they live. It is hard to say whether this is John's Bethany family. Neither Luke nor John answers the questions we might want to ask: Why are neither of the sisters married? How old are they and Lazarus? Are their parents still alive? Perhaps John's community knows them, or knows of them, and if so, the bare details in the story would be sufficient.

Healing stories are common enough in the Gospels, but the raising of the dead is relatively rare. The synoptic Gospels record the raising of Jairus' daughter (Mark 5:21-43 and parallels). Luke adds the raising of a widow's only son at Nain in Galilee (Luke 7:11-17). The raising of Lazarus is the longest and richest account of its kind in the Gospels. Alongside the obvious emotional impact of losing a much-loved family member, there are economic consequences. Lazarus, like the widow of Nain's son, may have been the source of income and security for women whose bereavement now faces them with the prospect of destitution. There are social consequences too. In their world, death is not private. The whole village gathers round. The sisters expect close friends like Jesus to come and offer support. There may well have been good reasons for his delay. His disciple Thomas certainly seems to sense the growing risk from the rising tide of hostility (John 11:16; see 10:31-40). But the sisters' reputation is hardly enhanced when a trusted family friend fails to turn up for the funeral.

Though he is the focus of attention, Lazarus says nothing, either before his death or after his raising. In what follows I concentrate on Mary, despite Martha being the one who confesses her faith in Jesus. Here I follow the lead of the evangelist, who in his introduction to the story tells us something about Mary that is clearly important to him: 'Mary was the one who anointed the Lord with perfume and wiped his feet with her hair' (11:2). After the raising of Lazarus, Jesus returns to Bethany and the hospitality of his special friends (12:1-7), in the altogether happier circumstances of a meal, though not without sinister background noises (11:45-57). John uses Mary's anointing to sign off her family's encounter with Jesus, and to bring his audience to the threshold of the second part of his Gospel, the narrative of Jesus' passion.

There seems to be some cross-pollination from the other Gospels in John's anointing story. Luke 7:36-39 has an anonymous 'woman of the city, who was a sinner' (often mistakenly identified as Mary Magdalene) anoint Jesus' feet with ointment and tears, only to wipe them with her hair, while he is eating at the house of Simon the Pharisee. Mark 14:3-9 also has Jesus anointed by an unnamed woman, but this time he is enjoying the hospitality of Simon the leper in Bethany. Like Mary of Bethany, she uses 'costly ointment of pure nard', but she anoints Jesus' head, not his feet. Whatever lies behind John's account, he uses these links to suggest that Mary's response to Jesus is motivated by generous, even extravagant, love, in a gesture that anticipates Jesus' washing the disciples' feet, which itself is so heavy with symbolism of even greater love (John 13:1-20; 15:12, 13).

I imagine Mary telling of her disappointment at Jesus' delayed response to the news of her brother's illness, her reaction to him when he eventually arrives, and her very different response to Jesus at the supper in their house just a few days before Passover.

Mary's story

Our brother died so quickly. His illness came so suddenly. It didn't seem five minutes since the three of us were celebrating the Sabbath with our friends and neighbours. By the time it ended, he was feeling unwell. Then he took to his bed. We cared for him ourselves at first, then we asked a doctor to help. But he was getting worse. We heard that Jesus wasn't far away, so we sent for him. But he arrived too late. By the time he showed up, Lazarus was dead and buried.

What would we do now? Martha and I were getting no younger. Lazarus was our life. Our future.

When Jesus eventually arrived, I still wasn't thinking straight. 'Why didn't you come straight away?' He must have known we wouldn't ask for help if it wasn't so urgent. 'It's not like you to keep your distance. You're our closest friend. We know the risks. We understand the dangers. But you could still have come sooner. You could have travelled after dark. You didn't have that far to come.'

He wasn't there when our brother was so ill. He still wasn't there when we buried him. We were mystified. We knew what some people were thinking. We've lived in Bethany long enough. Of course no one said anything to our faces, but we didn't have to read their lips to work it out. 'Their great friend Jesus didn't come when they sent for him. He didn't even arrive in time for the funeral. What kind of family are they, if their best friend doesn't show up when they need him?'

We'd always trusted Jesus. We'd always been very close. When Lazarus died, it felt like we'd lost everything. Our brother, our future, our reputation. Had we lost Jesus' friendship too? Was that why he took his time?

I can still remember what I said to him when Martha told me he'd arrived and wanted to see me:

> The house is full again, Jesus,
> but not because you're here.
> People are wondering where you are.
> Wondering what kept you away.
> You.
> Our friend.
> Our brother's friend.
> Everybody knows how much you loved him.
> He's dead, Jesus. Four days dead.
> The house is full again, Jesus.
> Full of death.

'It's not as bad as you think.' That was the message we got. 'It's all for the glory of God,' he said from a distance. What could possibly be so glorious about the death of your best friend? That's what I wanted to know when Jesus finally showed up, after Lazarus had been four whole days in the tomb. I was so exhausted by my jumbled-up feelings. All I could do was fall at his feet:

> I can't stop crying, Jesus.
> I don't know where I am.
> Except I'm here at your feet
> telling you what you already know.
> My brother should still be alive.
> Jesus, you should have come
> as soon as you heard.

It wasn't long before Jesus was back in Bethany at the supper we gave just before Passover. Martha and I still hadn't got used to Lazarus being around when we got up in the morning. I listened for his breathing when I woke up in the night. I was afraid that every day would be like one of those dreams where your deepest wishes come true, and then you wake up to find nothing's changed.

I couldn't say what I felt at the supper, so I let my body do the talking:

> Oil for the head.
> Water for the feet.
> That's how we greet our guests.
> But for you, Jesus, something else.
> The finest, costliest oil.

Our perfumed burial oil.
Oil we last used on Lazarus' dead body.
Oil for your feet.
How extravagant, someone says.
Such a waste.
I let the grumbling wash over me
as the oil of death fills the house
with the heady fragrance of love.

How John uses the story of Mary the sister of Lazarus

The Prologue's bold assertion, 'in him was life' (1:4), reaches its climax in this sixth of Jesus' signs. It recalls John's account of the second sign in 4:46-54, with a boy whom Jesus neither knew nor met on the brink of death. His word – help given to strangers as soon as it was requested – proved powerful enough to revive the lad from a distance. Lazarus slipped over the edge in Bethany, with Jesus absent despite being summoned by those he loved. Yet the words he eventually spoke into his close friend's fourth day of darkness could hardly have been more animating.

In the story of the Bethany family, the evangelist changes gear to slow down his narrative, spreading the events of the remaining eight chapters over as many days. The accompaniments of Lazarus' recovery – surprise, an empty tomb, the mention of grave clothes, an air of celebration – hint at the end of the Gospel, but Jesus' passion looms large enough to prevent any premature exuberance. Threats against his life intensify, as the authorities decide that the consequences of Jesus' action leave them with no option but to have him killed (11:45-53). Even Lazarus is no longer safe (12:9-11). His recovery makes the Passover crowds even more volatile. Jesus is carried on a wave of excitement into Jerusalem, where he will act out the descent and ascent of the Word made flesh (12:20-35).

Jesus' remark in 11:4 that Lazarus' illness is for the glory of God and his Son may seem at first to trivialise his and his sisters' suffering, especially if it is read as a generalising comment. It is better to read it alongside the retrospective statements that regularly appear in John's narrative, which suggest that deeper meanings only become apparent with the benefit of hindsight and the help of the Holy Spirit (2:22, 12:16, 14:26). Not every illness is glorious, and some are anything but. Lazarus' illness has its particular quality because of the chain of events it triggers, though this could hardly have been evident in the forward movement of things. Only with a backwards view is its deeper meaning disclosed.[44] This certainly injects a sense of realism into the Bethany

---

44. 'Life can only be understood backwards; but it must be lived forwards', in Soren Kierkegaard, *Journals IV A 164 (1843)*, London: Penguin Classics. A Selection, 1996.

story that can only benefit the evangelist's audience. Like Lazarus and his family, their anxieties are exacerbated by the physical absence of Jesus and the stubborn persistence of the death that results from their enemies' hostility as well as natural causes. John's hope-filled narrative does not remove the painful realities of death and loss, but encourages them to stand firm in the face of them.

The resurrection of the dead is a key element in Christianity's language of hope. At the time of Jesus, it was a relative newcomer to Jewish faith, where it appeared as an overture to the day of judgement. Early Christian writers like Paul and John understandably shifted the emphasis towards resurrection as the renewal of all things in Christ, including the vindication of Jesus and the possibility of continuing communion with him. The New Testament does not provide a carefully constructed doctrine of an afterlife, more a set of variations on a common theme. Jesus' life beyond the violent death he suffered represents God's desire to bring his good creation to its full and final purpose, but only as a definitive deposit rather than the full payment. Early Christian hope includes elements of 'now' and 'not yet'. Some New Testament writings emphasise the 'not yet' of resurrection in order to guard against the over-confidence that comes from believing that God's future has already arrived (this is the case in 1 Thessalonians 5 and 1 Corinthians 15). But sometimes the 'now' needs highlighting because confidence is low and hope is disappointed (as in Ephesians, Colossians and Hebrews). The Gospel of John tends towards the 'now' end of the spectrum. Those who believe in Jesus as the embodiment of God's love for the world already have eternal life (3:16). Believers who eat the bread of life at the banquet of Sophia-Logos will not die but live for ever, yet only because they will be raised up on the last day (6:39, 50, 51). So the evangelist does not lose sight of the 'not yet' dimension of hope. In 5:28, Jesus speaks of an hour that is coming 'when all who are in their graves will hear [the] voice' of the Son of God. Lazarus' emergence from his tomb points ahead to this resurrection on the 'last day' (11:24), for which he too must wait, and learn to live with the prospect of a second funeral.

According to John, Jesus-shaped hope inhabits and transforms the 'now' of human experience, even the ever-present realities of death and loss. But such hope can never be fully captured by the 'now'. There is always more; however rich the present moment may be, it is only ever provisional.

Reflections

Love is one of the threads that runs through the story of the Bethany family. Lazarus and his sisters are introduced in 11:3-5 as beloved disciples, and Jesus' love for them eventually overcomes the risk of falling into the hands of his enemies in Jerusalem. Love gives life-giving power to the words Jesus speaks into Lazarus' tomb, and Mary's extravagant anointing can only be the response of love.

The love we find in this story is forged by the realities of vulnerability, disappointment and loss. It has a mysterious quality which makes it hard at times to grasp or predict. In her poem 'Love, Like Water', Julia Copus sees love 'wearing the deepest of grooves in our sides / and filling them up again, ever so gently / wounding us, making us whole'.[45] Her suggestion that wholeness is not possible without love's wounding effect exposes the vulnerability and ambiguity of love. Its active power in the world, however gentle and sensitive, shapes and even wounds what it encounters. Yet this is how love makes us whole, says the poet. At times we may experience God's love as a lake being hollowed out, a deep groove being worn in us. This may mystify, disappoint, even enrage us. Yet at Bethany, the wounds are made 'ever so gently', only to be filled with God's unimaginable gift.

How does Julia Copus' image of 'love, like water' help you to reflect on the different experiences of the characters in the Bethany story?

45. Julia Copus, 'Love, Like Water', in her collection *In Defence of Adultery*, Tarset, Northumberland: Bloodaxe Books, 2003.

TWELVE

Philip

John 12:20-36

Background

Philip is named in all the lists of the disciples in the Gospels and Acts, though he has a more prominent place in John's Gospel. In the synoptic Gospels, Peter, James and John form the inner core of the twelve. Not so in John, who mentions Philip alongside Simon Peter and Andrew. In John 1:35-51, Philip is one of the Galileans whom Jesus meets among the disciples of John the Baptiser, and the first to whom Jesus says, 'follow me'. Having been found by Jesus, he goes on to find Nathanael, another of the baptiser's disciples, and invites him to 'come and see' Jesus. In 6:1-14, faced with a large, hungry crowd by the Sea of Galilee, Jesus tests Philip by asking him how they might be fed. Philip's rather obvious point about the prohibitive cost of buying each of them a mere mouthful of bread only highlights the contrast between the insufficiency of what can be bought and the abundance of what is given. In 12:20-22, some Greek-speaking pilgrims in Jerusalem for Passover seek out Philip and ask him to arrange an introduction to Jesus, which he does, though Jesus' response is enigmatic. Philip's final appearance comes in 14:1-11, at the supper Jesus shares with his disciples at the same festival. Philip and Thomas manage to tease out what Jesus means when he speaks about knowing the Father through him. In all these episodes, it appears that Philip's role as a disciple is to pave the way for revelation.

Twice John reveals that Philip, like Simon and his brother Andrew, is from Bethsaida, at the northern end of the Sea of Galilee (1:44, 12:21). Bethsaida was not far from the border between the Roman provinces of Galilee and Golan. Like many such towns, it belonged first to one province and then another as the border shifted, which it did between the time of Jesus and John's Gospel, moving east to take the town into Galilee. According to the Jewish historian Josephus, Galilee was an essentially rural region, with peasant villages surrounded by a circle of Greek-style cities on the periphery. This brought the inevitable urban/rural tensions, but also a high level of contact among its interdependent, ethnically mixed, multi-lingual population. The economy of Galilee was based on agriculture and fishing. Bethsaida was a thriving centre of the salted fish industry, with easy access to the towns around the lake and the markets further afield in the province of the Decapolis (Ten Cities), on the eastern side of the Jordan. According to Luke 10:13-15, Jesus was not welcomed in Bethsaida and the surrounding Galilean towns. Perhaps he censured them because their wealth was an impediment to the repentance he called for.

I imagine Philip, a native of Bethsaida in Galilee, as a disciple who is particularly open to the breadth of Jesus' revelation. This in turn makes him a ready point of contact for those whose desire to see Jesus draws them from the edges of the Jewish world and beyond.

Philip's story

Bethsaida is where I'm from. So many worlds meet in my small town. Fishing is big here. We catch fish and salt them. Then sell them far and wide. We do a lot of farming too. We trade across the lake, and with Syria and Lebanon to the north, and the Ten Cities to the east. So many voices in the streets of Bethsaida, so many tongues. Aramaic and Hebrew, the languages of my people. Greek and Latin, the languages of the empire. So much movement, so many contacts. So much prosperity, yet the poor are always with us. It's easy to feel in Bethsaida that the whole world is drawn to our doorstep.

My world is bigger than Bethsaida. I go regularly to Jerusalem for the festivals of our people. There I hear many more languages. Abraham's children are scattered far beyond the land God promised. They come from east and west, north and south to celebrate and remember and renew their hope. I come to the city now with Jesus of Nazareth. I met him in Bethany beyond the Jordan, not in Galilee or Jerusalem as you might expect. I'd gone there to listen to John the baptiser, because once when I was in Jerusalem it seemed like everybody was talking about him. I met some Galileans among his followers. Andrew and Simon, Nathanael from Cana. When I say that I met Jesus, it makes it sound as if it was my doing. The truth is that he found me, and he called me to follow him – and Andrew and Simon and Nathanael too.

When I came back to Galilee with him, I found my world growing even bigger. Jesus lived as if borders didn't exist. I don't think he saw them. If he did, they didn't seem to matter. As far as he was concerned, boundaries were for crossing, not holding people back. And slowly, those of us who were close to him learned to see the world through his eyes.

Last time I was in Jerusalem with Jesus, it turned out to be our final Passover together. I was approached by some Greek-speaking Jews who were visiting the synagogue where I worshipped whenever I was there. They told me they'd heard about Jesus. 'We'd like to see him,' they said. 'We want to know more about your rabbi.' So I found my friend Andrew, and together we took them to Jesus. A crowd had gathered round him as usual, to listen to his teaching. I was surprised at first by what he said to the Greeks. Lots of riddles and pictures – nothing new there – but there was an ominous tone in his voice, something I wasn't really expecting at the time. 'What is there to see in me? An hour that has all but arrived; a single seed falling into the ground and dying to produce the harvest; the Son of Man being lifted up in glory. If you really want to see me, then follow me, serve me, let go of your life, hate it. That's the only way you'll find God's blessing.' I'm not sure what the Greeks made of it, though he did say he'd draw the whole world – the world beyond Bethsaida and Jerusalem and Rome and the Great Sea – to himself when he was lifted up.

What Jesus said clearly affected him. I'd never seen him so disturbed. His words, his appearance completely changed the atmosphere. We'd gone to Passover as we always did, to remember Moses and our ancestors, to celebrate the way God freed them from slavery in Egypt, to hope that our liberation wouldn't be long in coming. How would we sing the songs of freedom after this? I remember the sky that day. It was very heavy with thunderclouds, almost dark by early afternoon. It was only a matter of time before the heavens opened. When Jesus spoke, it was like God's words were thundering all around us. I thought about Noah's flood and Moses going up Sinai and Elijah on Horeb. Thunder – the voice of God, the message of an angel – telling us all, not just the Greeks, to listen to the words of Jesus.

Some people in the crowd started arguing with Jesus. They said that if God's messiah was from heaven, he couldn't possibly die. But this was no time for quarrelling. The sky was growing darker by the minute. The light was fading fast. Jesus was sounding more and more urgent. 'Walk in the light while you can,' he shouted. 'It won't be with you much longer. Don't let the darkness overtake you. Believe what I say and become children of light. Refuse me, and you only have the darkness to look forward to.'

How John uses the story of Philip

John uses Philip as a witness to God's ever-widening revelation in Jesus. In Judea, in the company of John the Baptiser and those who are looking for a new future for God's people, Philip tells Nathanael that he and his friends from Bethsaida have found 'Jesus, the son of Joseph from Nazareth', the one whom the law and the prophets speak of. Nathanael overcomes his initial cynicism about Nazarenes, and acknowledges Jesus as 'the Son of God, the King of Israel'. But then Jesus opens the eyes of these Galileans still wider. He is more than a rabbi from Nazareth, even more than the fulfilment of Jewish hope. Jesus not only pushes back the boundaries between the Jewish and Gentile worlds, but between earth and heaven too. John's account of his first episode including Philip ends with an allusion to Jacob's dream of a ladder that allowed angels to move between earth and heaven (Genesis 28:10-17). 'Very truly, I tell you, you will see heaven opened and the angels of God ascending and descending upon the Son of Man' (1:51). The patriarch's dream of 'the house of God, the gate of heaven' becomes a reality in the dwelling place of Sophia-Logos who opens up the life of God.

The belief that Jesus is 'more than' the eye can see comes across again in the feeding of the great crowd in 6:1-14. When Jesus discusses with Philip and Andrew how a large crowd of Galileans might be fed, it is clear that buying bread is not an option. Somehow, in the hands of Jesus the food that a lad gives becomes more than enough. So who is this Jesus? The crowd see him as the answer to their hopes of a prophet promised by Moses, or even the one who would deliver them from their present slavery under Roman occupation. But as the story unfolds, Jesus is revealed as one who is more than a prophet whose attempts to feed the hungry are undaunted by meagre resources. He nourishes not just hungry Galileans with bread they would otherwise have to buy, but the life of the whole world with his freely-given flesh and blood at Sophia's banquet. Again, a story featuring Philip opens up the promise of heavenly sustenance, not just earthly bread, to the world beyond Galilee.

Philip's next appearance takes this 'more than' theme further. In 12:20-26, the Greeks who are in Jerusalem for Passover are more likely to be Greek-speaking Jews than Gentiles. Philip of Bethsaida has grown up with people like them. He speaks their language, so they naturally seek his favour. They want to see Jesus – and John's audience knows well enough by now that there is more to seeing than having eyes that work well. These Greeks want to believe in Jesus and to become his followers. Jesus' answer seems oblique at first, but then we hear words that are familiar from the synoptic Gospels about what it means to be a disciple. Loving life or hating it, losing life or keeping it for eternal life sum up the paradoxical promise of Jesus. The blessings of God's reign can only be received by those who are prepared to deny their own natural claim on life when confronted by one who is more than they imagine (see Mark 8:34-38 and parallels). To see Jesus, then, is to serve him, which means following him and sharing in the honour he receives from his Father.

But there is yet more to seeing Jesus, as sayings peculiar to John spell out. The Greeks are invited to 'see' more than a Jewish rabbi in full flow, with attentive and questioning disciples at his feet. 'See me as a seed falling into the ground and dying, as its hard outer shell is cracked open by the earth's moisture so that it can take root and grow.' This is John's language of grace, the descent of Sophia-Logos in the flesh-and-blood earthiness of God's Son, before returning in the 'hour' of his ascent into glory.

The road to glory is anything but glorious. In words that echo the other Gospels' accounts of Jesus' transfiguration and his prayer in Gethsemane (both missing from this Gospel), Jesus is deeply troubled by his hour, as well he might be. If his descent from heaven is like the seed falling into the ground and dying, then his ascent into heavenly glory is the hour of his 'lifting up' on the cross. These everyday images of planting seed in the earth and executing criminals a few feet above ground level reveal Jesus as the gate of heavenly glory, God's gift of the bread of life for the whole world.

The Greeks may still want to see Jesus, but others in the crowd have their doubts. If the scriptures say that the messiah lives for ever after inaugurating God's reign (though John gives no hints about which scriptures they have in mind), how can Jesus speak like this? Not for the first time are his audience left to work through their questions, as demanding as listening for a heavenly voice in a clap of thunder, with the light fading and the storm clouds gathering. If you still want to 'see' Jesus, says the evangelist to his audience, take advantage of the light in his words while there is still time. John's typical either/or view of the world leaves the eternal darkness of God's judgement as the only alternative.

John's final story featuring Philip, in 14:1-11, takes the 'more than' theme still further, as he recapitulates his opening account of Philip's call. At the beginning, Jesus spoke of seeing heaven opened. Now he speaks of seeing the Father. Thomas and Philip play the familiar Johannine role of disciples who struggle to make sense of Jesus, yet they manage to draw out his meaning. Jesus has been addressing the disciples' anxiety at the sense of abandonment his death will bring. He assures them that they have nothing to fear. His impending departure will take him to 'my Father's house', where he will 'prepare a place for you', before returning to 'take you to myself'. By now they should know that his execution is nothing less than the way to the Father's glory. But the message has not sunk in. Hence Thomas' 'we do not know where you are going; how can we know the way?'

In the Bible, 'the way' is an image of God's coming to redeem his people along the desert highway to their exile in Babylon (see Isaiah 40:3-5). In the Wisdom traditions, Sophia's way leads to salvation, especially in the exodus story in Wisdom 10:17, 18. In the synoptic Gospels, though not in John, the baptiser uses this metaphor of his own ministry (see Mark 1:2, 3 and parallels). Jewish renewal movements preparing for God's coming, such as the community at Qumran and the Jesus movement, also thought of themselves as 'the way' (see Acts 9:2; 19:23). In true Johannine fashion, Jesus applies these collective images of God's people and the coming of the saviour God to himself, in his 'I am the way, the truth and the life.' His disciples understandably see crucifixion as anything but the way to God's blessing. They have been taught by Deuteronomy 21:23 that a body hanging from a tree was a sign of God's curse. There must be some other way for Jesus to reveal the Father to them. Hence Philip's plea: 'Lord, show us the Father, and we shall be satisfied.'

Jesus goes on to assure them that what they see in the way of the cross is far more than shame and humiliation. It can only be the way to the Father. 'Those who have seen me have seen the Father', because 'I am in the Father and the Father is in me'. Once again Jesus draws on the poetry of Sophia-Logos to picture the mutual indwelling of Father and Son. Philip and the others can dare to believe that they see heaven opened where they least expect it: in Jesus-Sophia's invitation to eat my bread and drink my blood, in the Son of Man's burial in the earth like a grain of wheat, and in his lifting up a few feet above the ground in the hour of his exaltation.

John the evangelist uses the stories that feature Philip to show that Jesus is more than a rabbi who attracts his own followers, more than a long-expected prophet or messiah sent to redeem the children of Abraham, and certainly more than an irritant who has to be crucified to preserve the political status quo. To spell out the substance of this 'more than', John uses the most personal and intimate language available to him. 'Have I been with you so long, and yet you do not know me, Philip? Those who have seen me have seen the Father.' Every conceivable boundary is pushed back. Heaven is opened in the most unlikely way to Galileans and Judeans, Greeks and more. In the shared-out bread, the planted seed and the raised-up criminal, nothing less than the human face of God[46] is revealed for the whole world to see.

Reflections

There is rich symbolism in the material associated with Philip. Some of it is used to picture the reality of God: the open gate of heaven, the Father's house, the voice of God in what sounds like thunder. Other language is earthy and everyday: bread, seed planted in the ground, execution, going and coming, the way. The symbolism of heaven and earth comes together in the image of Jesus' being 'lifted up' on the cross, which invites those who want to 'see' Jesus to look in the most unexpected place. The execution symbol informs all the others. So bread and seed are not simply about spiritual nourishment, but life that is given, laid down, buried. Access to the heavenly realm is along the unlikely and demanding way of the cross. Walking the way of Jesus really does take us deeper into God.

Some people are more naturally sensitive than others to the power of symbolism to communicate the divine reality that is beyond our ordinary sight. Even those who are more at home with symbols find that it takes time for them to do their work. Symbols invite us to return to them again and again, to still ourselves and practise being attentive to what they reveal in the present moment.

If this is something familiar to you, choose one of the symbols from the Philip stories and live with it for a few days. Let it do its work by opening you up to the reality and call of God. If you are less confident with symbols, try carrying a small, significant object around with you for a while, and let it speak to you in its own way as you make

---

46. The title of John Robinson's study of Jesus (London: SCM Press, 1973).

yourself aware of it during the day. As you become more practised and confident, try working with other symbols: a picture or an image, silence, something from the world of nature, a lighted candle.

When you feel at home in the company of symbols, go back to the Philip stories and choose one from there. Live with it for a few days and be aware of where it leads your thinking, emotions and actions, as you say with the Greeks who searched out Philip, 'we want to see Jesus'.

THIRTEEN

Judas

John 12:1-8; 13:1-30

Background

Judas is an enigmatic figure. He is one of Jesus' chosen twelve, mentioned in all the lists of the disciples. Yet he is tarred forever by the brush of betrayal. Part of the difficulty in understanding Judas is that the Greek word paradidomai can simply mean 'hand over' as well as 'betray'. The first is morally neutral; the second suggests treachery. Was Judas putting Jesus in a place where he could confront his enemies directly, and so (at least in his own mind) doing his friend a favour? Or was he being utterly disloyal?

The Gospel accounts of Judas are all written from the perspective of hindsight. Whatever his motives, Judas' actions precipitated the arrest of Jesus and his subsequent execution. But there is enough variation in the way the evangelists tell the story of Judas to suggest that those who were close to him found it difficult to reach a unanimous verdict. Apart from his inclusion in the list of the twelve disciples, Judas appears for the first time in Mark's Gospel in 14:10, 11, where he approaches the chief priests with a view to handing Jesus over to them. Mark has earlier indicated that the authorities want to seize Jesus with a minimum of fuss, to avoid provoking a riot. Judas' insider information on the whereabouts of Jesus is well worth the reward they promise him. Matthew has Judas asking the authorities for money in advance, and they give him 30 pieces of silver. Luke sees Satan at work in Judas' clandestine conversations.

John uses these various elements to construct an altogether more sinister character. Where Matthew and Mark are content to have unnamed disciples grumbling at the sheer waste of anointing Jesus with very expensive ointment, John names the grumbler as Judas, whose supposed concern for the poor is a cover for his greed (12:6). Interestingly, John says nothing about Judas being rewarded for his betrayal. He is more interested in Judas as an instrument of Satan. As early as 6:70, Jesus identifies him as demonic, a true child of the murderous father of lies (8:44). John begins his account of the Passover meal with the reminder that Satan is at work in Judas (13:2). When he leaves the meal table to betray Jesus to the authorities, John has Judas going out into the night, symbolising the darkness of those who oppose him (13:30). When Jesus is arrested in 18:1-12, Judas brings armed soldiers and temple police. There is no need for a kiss to identify his master: Jesus speaks up for himself. John leaves no room for Matthew's account of Judas' remorse and suicide (Matthew 27:3-5), or even Luke's alternative version of his death in Acts 1:16-19. Judas disappears from the narrative, presumably into the darkness of God's judgement.

My interpretation of Judas involves some reading against the grain of John's Gospel. I imagine him being excited by the political overtones of some of Jesus' sayings recorded in this Gospel. 'I am the bread of life' harks back to one of Israel's foundational narratives, with Moses leading God's people through the wilderness, where they feast on manna, heavenly food for a people on the road to freedom. 'I am the good shepherd' picks up the critique of Israel's false shepherds in Jeremiah 23 and Ezekiel 34. These are rulers who look only to their own interests and lead the flock of God's people astray. These prophets look to God the true shepherd, and his promise to install another David as shepherd over his people. Jesus' words about bread and shepherds would have fired the hopes of men like Judas that he was the man to return Israel to the world of his namesake, Judas Maccabaeus, who had liberated Judea from foreign rule and purified the temple two centuries earlier. I see Judas motivated by his (in John's eyes, misguided) insistence that Jesus should take his own words seriously, and take steps to realise this popular vision of the history of God's covenant people.

Judas' story

I hoped I'd be able to slip out of the meal without anyone noticing. There's always a lot of coming and going at Passover. And someone always forgets something we need for the meal. By the time I left I needed fresh air as well as more food. Was I the only one? So much has been going on as we've travelled to the city for this year's festival. Take Lazarus and his sisters for example. Do we go to Bethany? Or do we stay where it's safe? Jesus didn't seem to know. First we were staying put. The next minute we were on the road. Our brother Thomas wasn't the only one to question what Jesus was up to.

Jesus is our leader, after all. A gifted rabbi, full of compassion – no one denies that. Some of us have been wondering for a while whether there's more to him. Much more. 'The Good Shepherd,' he said. 'I am the Good Shepherd.' You don't have to be a genius to work that one out. Think Jeremiah, think Ezekiel – two of our greatest prophets. 'Woe to the shepherds who destroy and scatter the sheep of my pasture, says the Lord.' 'The shepherds have fed themselves and not the sheep, so I will come and seek out my sheep.' 'The days are coming when I will raise up for David a righteous branch and he shall reign as king and deal wisely.'

How long have we been waiting for God to come like a shepherd, and get rid of the self-interested band of brigands we now have for leaders? How long do we have to wait for a shepherd like David to come and lead our people to freedom?

'The Bread of Life' was something else Jesus talked about. 'I am the Bread of Life.' He said it in the synagogue up in Galilee after he'd fed a great crowd of people. That was at Passover too. Some people wanted to make him king there and then. 'Is this the new Moses?' they were asking. 'Will Jesus lead us to freedom in our own promised land?'

Every time he raises the hopes of people like me for a better world, he seems to pull back, or go off in a different direction. Every time he challenges these double-dealing leaders we've got in Jerusalem, he disappears before we can put pressure on them to do something different. They're not interested in our freedom. Only in themselves, and their place in the Romans' pecking order.

I really snapped at Bethany, the meal we had a few days ago with Lazarus and his sisters. Why did she waste all that expensive perfume on Jesus' feet? He'd already had them washed – we all had. With water, like we always do when we're travelling. So why the burial oil? It costs a small fortune. If they didn't want it, they could have sold it and spent the money on feeding the poor. There's enough of them around at the moment, what with the price of bread and the taxes we have to pay. But don't waste it on his feet, please!

'Jesus,' I wanted to say, 'we need to be on our feet, not pampering them. It's Passover, and the crowds are with you, more than ever since you raised Lazarus. We can really do something this time to put some pressure on our so-called authorities to show these foreigners that we've had enough of being hungry.' I'm not stupid enough to think that we can get rid of the Romans. They're too powerful. There's too many of their soldiers in the city. But if we put some pressure on our ruling council, got them to see that we could make things difficult for them if they weren't prepared to act in their own people's interests for a change, maybe things could be different.

I thought Jesus needed a bit of pressure too. He's not going to behave like the good shepherd and the bread of life without a little help. He's not going to get them to see they have to be better shepherds, or else! I've been thinking for a while about setting up some kind of confrontation, but how, where? Then the penny dropped. Passover is the ideal time. The atmosphere is so volatile all it needs is a tiny spark and the whole lot will go up. Our shepherds wouldn't like that at Passover. The place is on high alert. You can't move for troops. They know what the Romans would do at the first sign of trouble.

So come on, Jesus the good shepherd – just make these self-servers realise how your people feel. How hungry we are, how sick we are of paying taxes to foreigners, how fed up we are of being slaves in the land that God promised to us! That's why I told the temple police where Jesus would be tonight after the meal. We always go to that garden across the Kidron valley whenever we're in the city. It's quiet – but not tonight. They've arrested him. They'll take him to our leaders. There's enough of us to make trouble. The city is full of

Galileans up for Passover. Some of us are carrying weapons. I'm not saying we should use them. But they need to know how strongly we feel that things have to be different. We want this to be our promised land. We're hungry for the bread of life. We're ready to follow the good shepherd.

How John uses the story of Judas

John writes a Gospel of polarities. He puts grace and law, light and darkness, life and death, truth and lies at opposite ends of the spectrum. People either see or they are blind. They are either Jesus' friends or his enemies. Jesus divides opinion sharply. From his first appearance in the company of John the Baptiser and his disciples, those who are invited to 'come and see' make up their minds about him very quickly. Nicodemus and his kind – torn between the competing loyalties of the synagogue and the Christ-followers – are deemed to lack the courage to come out of the shadows. And Jesus' more outspoken enemies are what they are because they are children of the devil.

As a man whose motives may have been mixed, Judas is both a challenge to John and a gift. The evangelist looks back at his *paradidomai* and sees only the most diabolical disloyalty. Here is a man whose avarice wants to measure a joyful woman's extravagance by the price of her ointment. In John's eyes he is a true embodiment of the deceitful and death-dealing character of evil, exchanging the fellowship of his friends for the company of their enemies. He goes from the supper into the night, only to emerge in the garden at the head of an armed squad of Roman soldiers and temple police. Jesus is led away to the powerbrokers of Jerusalem and Rome, before being condemned to death. But Judas is condemned to something much worse: he disappears from the story, into the darkness of the judgement of God.

Clearly John has no sympathy for Judas. He is a greedy thief and an agent of darkness, who steals money and takes life. By contrast the one he betrays is full of generous, vulnerable love, who is prepared to risk his life for the sake of his friends, and opens himself to misunderstanding and even violence. Jesus and Judas are polar opposites, as far apart as light and darkness, each a foil to the other. And yet John needs his Judas figure to illustrate the perils of living in darkness. Judas is chosen by Jesus to be one of those he calls friends rather than servants. Yet he is the one member of the Jesus group in whom the uncertainties and anxieties that others have about Jesus are brought to the surface and given free rein. He is the shadow-side of discipleship, whose *paradidomai* shows what happens when a person's primary loyalty is to self-centred hopes rather than other-centred faith. In John's eyes, Judas could never have been driven by the moral neutrality of giving his friend a chance to speak up for himself, but only by the diabolical treachery of betrayal.

Reflections

One reason why Jesus and Judas are at opposite ends of the light-darkness spectrum is that they see the world completely differently. Their prejudices could not be more contradictory. Prejudice often makes us feel uneasy. It has all kinds of negative connotations. We may find ourselves claiming that, unlike 'them', 'we' are not prejudiced. But we all have our prejudices. Prejudice is no more than the judgements that inform our experience. Some of them are good, others not so. Our prejudices are not necessarily fixed, though they may be difficult to alter, depending on how deeply founded they are and how much they serve our vested interests. Even if we could remove all our negative judgements, we would not be able to eliminate prejudice. None of us sees life through empty eyes.

Roger McGough's poem 'You and I' is about the way the same actions can evoke strikingly different responses. 'I explain quietly. You / hear me shouting . . . I / am placatory. You / sense a new selfishness.'[47] Whatever I may intend or do, you see things differently. However you may think or act, I sense an ulterior motive.

Prejudice has something to do with what you and I bring to our experience, and how this shapes the way we sense and feel and interpret it. 'You and I' invites us to be honest about the way we see and judge. It also sheds light on the differences between the way Jesus and Judas behave at the two meals in John's Gospel.

> What you see as waste
> I want to welcome.
> What you view as indecision and prevarication
> I regard as faithful patience.

Jesus and Judas approach life with very different prejudices. Prejudice may well be more complex than John suggests, but the 'You and I' of the stories he tells about Jesus and Judas at the meal table invites us to reflect on the mix of light and darkness in what we bring to our everyday experience.

---

47. Available in *Waving at Trains*, London: Jonathan Cape, 1982, and *Collected Poems*, London: Viking, 2003.

FOURTEEN

Caiaphas
John 11:45-57; 18:1-14, 19-24

Background

Judea had been under direct Roman rule since AD 6, under the Roman governor based in Caesarea. Day-to-day governance was in the hands of the Sanhedrin, a group of senior priests and Pharisees led by a high priest appointed by the emperor. The Jewish rulers were responsible for paying the imperial taxes and keeping the peace. Rome tended to appoint and depose the high priest at will. Annas was appointed at the beginning of direct rule, and his five sons and grandson succeeded him. Caiaphas married into the family, and was appointed high priest in AD 18. He served until 37, when he was deposed by Pontius Pilate's successor. As the longest-serving high priest in the first Christian century, he worked closely with Pilate and brought stability to Judea.

In all four Gospels, Jesus is at odds with Jewish authorities. In the synoptic Gospels, his arguments are mainly with Pharisees in Galilee (sometimes they are sent from Jerusalem) and chief priests in Jerusalem. Issues come to a head when Jesus brings his vision of God's kingdom before the Jerusalem authorities at Passover. In the circumstances (a liberation festival with a city full of pilgrims, including a number who have travelled with Jesus), they have no option but to act against him. John's Gospel presents a more complex picture. Throughout his ministry, Jesus moves between Galilee and Jerusalem, which he visits as a pilgrim at the Jewish festivals. Disputes here are more protracted than in the other Gospels. We have seen how they arise out of his Sabbath-day healings, which raise questions about his authority. What gives him the right to act and speak as he does? Where does his authority come from? Where is he from? He draws enough of a following to take these arguments beyond the usual in-house debates among Jewish factions. Things come to a head after the raising of Lazarus, when Jesus' popularity is such that he is judged to pose a threat to the politics of compromise (11:48).

Today's readers naturally want to know what to make of the differences between John and the other Gospels here. They are partly the result of different narrative and historical concerns. The synoptic Gospels are interested in telling the story of Jesus' conflict with Jewish authorities outside Jerusalem, and the way this explodes in the climactic visit that had such dramatic consequences. John is more concerned to show how the final conflict took shape in Jerusalem itself, over a much longer period of time – throughout most of Jesus' ministry, from what we can gather. We might say that all four Gospels take different routes to the same destination. Does this make one account of the journey more factually true than the others, or are their differences complementary? Questions like these ensure that debates among readers at all levels continue.

When we look more closely at the Gospel accounts,[48] all four have Jesus brought before Jewish and Roman authorities for what are more likely to have been informal hearings than an official trial. There is much common ground among the Gospel writers, but some significant differences in the details. Matthew follows Mark in having the Jewish authorities question Jesus about his attitude to the temple (Luke omits this) before asking him whether he is the messiah. In Mark, Jesus answers with an unequivocal 'I am', but in Luke and Matthew he is more guarded: 'you say that I am'. All three synoptic Gospels have Jesus referring to the mysterious coming of the Son of Man, which his interrogators judge to be blasphemous. Jesus is then sent to Pilate, charged with holding the messianic aspiration to be 'the king of the Jews'. In John, the former high priest Annas questions Jesus about his teaching and his disciples, before sending him to Caiaphas (who asks him nothing) and then to Pilate, who asks the same question reported by the other Gospels: 'Are you the king of the Jews?'

Blasphemy was deeply offensive to Jews, but in Roman eyes it was not a capital offence. The Jewish authorities were aware that, like them, Rome was keen to keep the peace particularly at Passover, when thoughts were of Moses and freedom from foreign rule. The substance of the Jewish interrogation in the synoptic Gospels – the authority of Jesus to speak and act for God – is also found in John. Annas wants to be sure that Jesus presents a sufficient threat to law and order to justify execution at the hands of Rome. His interest in Jesus' teaching is more about authority than content. A self-styled prophet claiming God's backing, with enough of a following to ignite the volatile atmosphere of a liberation festival, would be not only offensive but dangerous. According to 11:49, Caiaphas has already made up his mind about Jesus after the popular reaction to the raising of Lazarus. All that remains is to persuade Pilate.

I imagine Caiaphas reflecting on his part in Jesus' arrest. He is a man whose loyalties pull him this way and that. He is loyal to the survival of his own people and their temple; loyal too to the Roman authorities and the necessary compromises of his position. But Caiaphas has no such loyalty to Jesus. The fact that he poses a significant threat to the delicate balance of power between Rome and Jerusalem means that Caiaphas is prepared to hand over a son of Abraham to be executed by the occupying power, with the humiliation and shame that brought on his own people.

---

48. Matthew 26:57-68; Mark 14:53-65; Luke 22:54-71; John 18:13-24.

Caiaphas' story

It's been going on for too long. We couldn't wait any longer. We had to act. It's Passover, and we all know what that means. Jerusalem full of pilgrims and hotheads from all over the world. Away from home. Remembering Moses. Celebrating victory over ancient enemies. Looking for freedom. Passions are already running high. You can smell it in the streets. We're all on edge, just hoping there'll be no trouble. At this time of year I have nightmares. One tiny spark of violence in this tinder-dry landscape and the whole lot goes up in flames. The Governor and his troops step in. Rome takes all this off us. And then what?

Jesus. Why couldn't he stay in Nazareth where he belongs? They say nothing good comes from Nazareth – well, he's living proof. I'm convinced he went out of his way to provoke us. I've nothing against anyone healing the sick. The more healers the better, I say. The temple courts are forever cluttered with cripples and blind people and beggars. On some days you can hardly move around the city. But why did he have to heal them on the Sabbath, and during the festivals when the place was crowded?

Take the man he healed by the Sheep Gate. He hadn't walked for 38 years. What difference would it have made to wait one more day? Or the blind beggar he told to go and wash in the pool of Siloam. That man had never seen in his whole life. Why couldn't he have waited until the Sabbath was over?

The Pharisees from the synagogues here are hot when it comes to keeping the law of Moses. Maybe a little too hot at times. I've tried talking to them, getting them to go easy over some of the regulations. But I can see their point where this Jesus was concerned. The Sabbath is the Sabbath. Being strict about it is one of those practices that make us who we are. There are things that can wait. Some things you just don't need to do on the Sabbath, especially in public.

But there was more to it than that. If Jesus had just been a troublemaker I'm sure we could have persuaded him to go elsewhere, back to where he came from. But he has followers. Most of them are not from this part of the country. I was told that a mob up in Galilee wanted to make him king after he fed a great crowd of people. These are some of the people who come down with him to the festivals. They hang on his every word. He has followers who live in Jerusalem too. They take his teaching back into our synagogues. They stir up trouble, just like he does. They're divisive. We don't need that at the moment. It's peace we want, not division.

The synagogue leaders told me what used to happen whenever they challenged him. They'd ask him to justify himself. He'd say it was obvious to those who love God that he was doing his Father's work. 'God is always working,' he'd say, 'even on the Sabbath.' Our rabbis asked him for witnesses who'd vouch for his authority. 'Why don't you take me seriously?' he'd ask. 'I have the two witnesses the law requires. Listen to John the Baptist, listen to Moses or Abraham.' And then he'd say, 'if you're not prepared to listen to them, look at the good I'm doing. Can't you see this is what God does?' Well, no, frankly. Would God disregard his own laws, and send somebody to speak against Abraham and Moses?

The synagogue officials told me that one of the most irritating things about Jesus was his habit of talking in riddles. You could never get a straight answer from the man. He'd speak about going away somewhere where no one could follow him. If only he'd go to the Greek-speaking synagogues around the great sea. Let them deal with him! Unfortunately, that's not what he meant. But he would never say what he did mean! Or he'd talk about where he comes from, as if that gave him the right to act as he did. But we all know where he comes from – Nazareth in Galilee – and according to the scriptures nobody worth listening to comes from up there. And on top of that there are the rumours about his family. He went on about God being his father, but who was his real father? Nobody knows.

It could get very unpleasant when Jesus turned on the leaders who questioned him. 'You're only interested in the honour people give you. You should be more concerned about what my Father thinks of you. If you were really Moses' disciples and the children of Abraham you'd trust me, instead of wanting to kill me.' Who could blame us for wanting to stone him? He wasn't above insulting us, saying that we're not children of Abraham but the devil, 'the father of lies' he calls him, 'a murderer from the very beginning' – all because we wouldn't follow him. Some of our Pharisees reckoned he must be mad or a Samaritan. He even claimed to be greater than Abraham, the mouthpiece of God himself, the son who knows his father's business and does his work for him. When he was challenged over healing the blind man on the Sabbath, what he said was blasphemous: 'the Father and I are one'. He was as good as making himself God, and at the same time turning his back on Moses.

It wouldn't have been so bad if people had treated him as a madman and ignored him. But he could be so persuasive. Some of our people were saying he's the prophet Moses spoke about, or even the messiah. Now that really worried us. I told the Sanhedrin, our ruling council, the more that gets out, the more we're all in trouble. Especially after people started saying he'd raised a dead man to life. That drew even bigger crowds. When he came into the city for this Passover, some of the pilgrims waved palm branches as if he was our king. And even some of our own people from Jerusalem joined in. The word was out that we were losing control, that it wouldn't be long before the Romans stepped in. I told the Sanhedrin, 'it's either him or us. We have him taken out, or the Romans will take us out.' They'd wreck our holy place and take control. It's happened before. It's what they do. Think of how much blood we'd have to spill to get back what freedom we have. Better to have one man die for our people than for everyone to suffer.

We had to act quickly. We decided to bring Jesus in, but we couldn't do it alone. We got a tip-off from one of his followers, telling us where he'd be. What price loyalty, eh? I went to see the Governor, and told him I might have a man for him to crucify. The Romans always have public executions at this time of year. They enjoy it, they say it keeps us under control. Normally I don't like seeing our own people on the wrong end of foreign violence. It shames us all. It shows how weak we really are. But this year I thought we could turn it to our advantage. I told Pilate that this blasphemer could make trouble for him too. I said he couldn't just sit back and give him his head during this Passover festival. It would be way too dangerous. And what would Caesar think if his Governor couldn't manage a little outpost of empire like Judea?

My plans seem to be working. The Governor lent us some of his soldiers in case Jesus and his followers made more trouble than our temple police could handle. But I gather they managed to arrest him without too much fuss. His followers were armed though, and one of them injured a servant of mine with his sword during the fracas. All this happened while I was still with Pilate, so Jesus was tied up and taken to Annas, my father-in-law. He asked him a few questions about his teaching and his followers. But he didn't get much out of him. Once I'd finished with Pilate, Jesus was brought to me. I didn't want to waste time interrogating him. What was the point? We knew he was trouble. We just wanted to be rid of him, and give his followers the strongest possible message that if they didn't clear off, the same would happen to them. So I sent Jesus to Pilate, as we agreed. He can deal with him now. And bring this troublesome Galilean to the end he deserves.

How John uses the story of Caiaphas

Behind John's account of Jesus' interrogation by the high priests lies an informal trial that has been running through his narrative since the healing of the paralysed man in chapter 5.[49] Though Caiaphas makes his first appearance in John's narrative after the raising of Lazarus, he and the other Jewish leaders have been kept well informed by Pharisees and other Jews about Jesus' teaching and activity, and his potential to disturb the peace (7:32, 11:46). The Jewish authorities twice try to have Jesus arrested (7:32, 10:39), and on two other occasions some members of the crowd are prepared to take the law into their own hands and stone him (8:59, 10:31). After the popular reaction to the raising of Lazarus, the Jewish leaders decide that Passover is too volatile a festival to allow Jesus free rein to stir up trouble.[50] With Judas'

---

49. See above on the healing of the paralysed man, pages 49-55.
50. In the synoptic Gospels, the impact of Jesus' entry into Jerusalem, his cleansing of the temple and his public teaching provokes official action.

help, they succeed in taking Jesus into custody (18:1-4), thus paving the way for his meeting with the deposed high priest Annas, before being taken to the current incumbent, his son-in-law Caiaphas.

John presents Caiaphas as a shrewd leader who is well aware of the issues raised by Jesus' presence in and around Jerusalem. His remarks after the raising of Lazarus show that he is well aware that his own status and authority are compromised. How does he protect his people, their beloved holy place that is entrusted to him, and his own privileged yet precarious position? He realises that Jesus challenges much more than the teaching authority of the Pharisees. He threatens the political stability of Jerusalem, especially as Passover approaches. His following is growing. Crowds are difficult to control at the best of times, but if a city full of pilgrims gets out of hand, the Roman governor will intervene, with dire consequences not only for a Jewish leadership that owes its position to a foreign power, but also for Israel's temple and government. 'Better to have one man die for the people than to have the whole nation destroyed' (11:50) is the judgement of political expediency.

John sees through the fudge surrounding Caiaphas to a deeper meaning in his judgement of Jesus. What he says makes him a prophet of the benefit that this troublemaker's death will bring not only to his own nation but the wider, dispersed Jewish people (11:52). These expressions of salvation are in line with traditional Jewish hopes for the restoration of God's people and the security of Jerusalem,[51] but there is more here than Caiaphas can possibly realise. The irony in his judgement is an invitation to consider its unintended surplus of meaning. Jesus is not just a dangerous irritant who needs to be flushed out of the body politic for the sake of its own health. In his death, John hears strong resonances with the ancient scriptural story of his people. Jesus is the much-loved sacrificed son who carries God's promise of universal blessing (3:16; see Genesis 22:1-19). He is the exalted source of healing (3:14; see Numbers 21:9), and the sustaining bread and water of life for a people on the way to freedom (6:1-59; 7:37-39; see Exodus 16:1-36; 17:1-7). He is the promised shepherd of Israel, who defeats their enemies not with weapons of war but by laying down his life freely (10:1-18; see Jeremiah 23; Ezekiel 34). He is the servant exalted in his sufferings, whose labours are rewarded in the light he brings to the nations (12:32; 13:1-20; see Isaiah 49:1-6; 52:13). He is the unblemished sacrificial Lamb of God, whose blood makes it possible for his people to be truly free (1:29; 19:14; see Exodus 12:1-38; Isaiah 53:7). And he is the righteous sufferer rejected by his own people, yet vindicated by the God in whom he trusts.[52]

---

51. See Isaiah 11:11; Jeremiah 23:3; 32:37; Ezekiel 34:11-16; Zechariah 14.
52. John weaves texts from Psalms 22, 69 and 34 into his account of Jesus' death between 19:24 and 19:37. They relate the experience of the righteous person, who suffers at the hands of his enemies and is vindicated by God.

Of course none of this would have been evident to Caiaphas. The resonances only appeared and grew stronger with the later need to make sense of Jesus' execution in a world that saw the crucified as shameful, weak and foolish. John, like other New Testament writers, searched the Jewish scriptures for ways of understanding Jesus' death in terms of God's good purposes for the world. None of the scriptural resonances has a sound that exactly matches the source, and occasionally texts have been re-shaped to improve their fit. But that is in keeping with the flexible approach that John and his contemporaries adopted towards the scriptures, so that they could detect enough of the ways of God in their stories to see them converging on the one whose death Caiaphas found so necessary.

When Jesus finally appears before Caiaphas, he has already been interrogated by his father-in-law Annas, in order to gauge the level of threat he presents. Jesus seems surprised at the inquiry into his teaching, and his response must have been sufficiently forthright for one of the arresting officers to hear it as disrespect for the authority of the high priest's office. Jesus refuses to be intimidated. He has more power than we might expect of a man who is under arrest, yet not enough to prevent his being passed from one Jewish official to another. When he finally reaches Caiaphas, the high priest has nothing to say. There is no need for any kind of trial. The high priest has already made up his mind. He simply hands Jesus over to Pilate, and entrusts the fate of Jerusalem and its Galilean troubler to a foreign official.

Reflections

John's account of Jesus before the high priests shows how he is carried along by powerful forces managed and sometimes manipulated by high-ranking men. But they too are under authority, and Caiaphas in particular is caught between the compromised and sometimes competing loyalties that enable him to maintain the status quo. His place in the politics of his day and in John's story invite further reflection on the way power is exercised in the world we know. Where do you see people like Caiaphas among today's leaders and powerbrokers? What compromises do you think they have to make in order to maintain the interests they represent? How do you and your church pray for them?

In Christian worship and theology, Jesus comes across as more than a victim of the self-interests of the leaders of his own people. But John makes it clear that he is not less than this. In this sense he is not unique. As the incarnation of Sophia-Logos in real flesh and blood, he inevitably shares his victimhood with others. Where and in whom do you see this dimension of his story continuing?

Pontius Pilate
John 18:28–19:22

Background

Pontius Pilate appears in all four Gospels as the Roman official who authorises the execution of Jesus. He was the prefect of the Roman province of Judea under the Emperor Tiberias between AD 26 and 36, when the province was under direct Roman rule. As prefect he lived in Caesarea, the provincial capital, and was mainly responsible for collecting the imperial taxes and conducting military operations, with about 3000 soldiers at his disposal across the province. He kept a low profile on his infrequent visits to Jerusalem, only going at the major feasts or at times of unrest and staying at the praetorium in Herod's palace on the western side of the city.

According to Jewish sources, Pilate was known for his furious temper, corruption, violence and insensitivity towards Jewish feelings. There are accounts of his offending the local population by allowing Roman standards to be brought into Jerusalem. He only had them removed under pressure, from the emperor on one occasion and the threat of martyrdom by protestors on another. He used the temple's money to build an aqueduct. The project was unpopular with the Jews, and Pilate suppressed a group of protestors by ordering his troops to surround them, before beating and killing them. He was ordered to return to Rome after violently suppressing an alleged Samaritan uprising in AD 36, and was replaced as prefect by Marcellus the following year.

The Gospels' accounts of Jesus' appearance before Pilate are broadly similar. The Jewish authorities are aware that they need to secure Pilate's interest in removing a man whose teaching and ability to cause unrest give them cause for concern. Pilate is unlikely to bother about the first, but the second belongs to the area of responsibility he shares with the Sanhedrin. Matthew and Mark have Jesus brought before Pilate after the Sanhedrin's informal hearings, which conclude that Jesus is guilty of blasphemy and deserves to die. Jesus is largely silent before Pilate and the continuing accusations of the Jewish leaders, much to Pilate's surprise. He only speaks in response to Pilate's question: 'Are you the king of the Jews?' Pilate is hardly enthusiastic in condemning Jesus, and is minded to release him – something his wife advises in Matthew's account, on the strength of a dream she has had about him. But he is persuaded by the demands of the crowds, whipped up by the chief priests, to crucify Jesus rather than another prisoner, Barabbas, whom he releases.

Luke gives a fuller account of Pilate's interrogation of Jesus. He makes the Sanhedrin's accusations explicit, and stages the hearings over three scenes to increase the dramatic tension. In scene one, the Jewish leaders accuse Jesus of 'perverting our nation, forbidding us to pay taxes to Caesar and saying that he himself is the Messiah, a king'. Pilate is interested only in the last charge, but he is not convinced that Jesus deserves to be crucified. Scene two shifts to Herod's residence. When Pilate learns that Jesus is a Galilean, he sends him to Herod, who is in Jerusalem for the Passover. Herod is equally unconvinced that there is enough evidence to convict Jesus, and sends him back to Pilate. In scene three, Pilate once again wants to release Jesus, and antagonises the assembled crowds as well as their leaders. Together they shout for his crucifixion, and Pilate tries a third time to release him. He finally accedes to the Jews' demands by releasing Barabbas and handing Jesus over to be crucified.

John's account expands Luke's three scenes into seven, and moves back and forth between the inside and outside of the praetorium. On the inside, Pilate interrogates Jesus alone and asks him whether he is the king of the Jews (presumably this is what the Jewish leaders mean when they accuse him of being a criminal). On the outside, Pilate deals with Jesus' accusers, telling them that there is insufficient evidence to crucify Jesus and offering to release him. The outcome is the same as in the other Gospels. Pilate eventually gives way to the demands of the leaders (John has no baying crowd to satisfy, only Jesus' accusers) and hands Jesus over to be crucified. But John's account is significantly different. On the inside and the outside of the praetorium, Pilate brokers a discussion of the relationship between the authorities that he, the Jewish leaders and Jesus each represent. Before Pilate, Jesus is no longer silent, and they discuss Johannine business: truth, where Jesus is from, the authority of this world and what lies above. Pilate is clearly disturbed by what he hears from Jesus. But before the Jews, Pilate is playful and manipulative. Only when he succeeds in forcing the Jewish leaders to acknowledge the authority of the emperor does he agree to their demands.

I imagine Pilate as the ruthless figure from the Jewish sources. He is irritated at having to be in Jerusalem at all, let alone deal with what might appear to be a local problem. But as his engagement with the Jewish leaders and their prisoner proceeds, he is both disturbed and increasingly frustrated. He takes the anxiety generated by his conversations with Jesus and uses it against his accusers. That way he and they can each indulge their delusions and see themselves as winners in their Passover-tide game.

Pontius Pilate's story

Do I enjoy my annual trip to Jerusalem for their Passover? I am not a Jew. Is that enough of an answer?

I come because I have to. I am Caesar's presence in this far-flung little patch of his world. I'm here because these Judeans need to know who's in charge. There's enough in their religion to feed the fantasies of a whole empire, let alone their measly city-state. They're not content to keep their god, Yahweh, to themselves and their temple. They want the whole world for him. Why we don't insist that they worship Caesar, like everyone else we've conquered, is beyond me. We should demolish their shrine instead of letting them re-build it. We let them come here in their thousands at this time of year to remember some ancient lawgiver who liberated their ancestors from slavery. It's an open invitation to sedition.

I've told Caesar he should put a stop to it. But I get the same response every time: 'You've got the troops, you've got the chariots and the swords. Get more of them in. Crucify a few Jews. There's nothing like public executions to keep occupied people in their place.' I suppose that's a good reason for coming to Jerusalem. I enjoy crucifixion. I don't get involved personally, of course – except that I give the orders. But Caesar is right. It shows who's in charge.

I usually know when I arrive in Jerusalem how many we'll be executing. Some of them will have been in prison, waiting for the big day. But this year I've been told there's a latecomer, Jesus from Nazareth. He's only just been arrested by their temple soldiers. They picked him up in some garden on the other side of the city. I don't know much about him. None of his followers was arrested – I'm told that one of them tipped him off to the authorities. Who needs enemies with friends like that? I told them to bring him to me once their council had finished with him. Here they are now.

I'm amused that these people won't come into my house if there's a festival on. They'll hand over one of their own to me, but they don't want to be tainted by stepping onto Roman soil. Except they're always on Roman soil, because it all belongs to us now. I can't make any sense of their mumbo-jumbo. But then, I don't need to. I'd rather play games with them.

We let them think they rule the place. Truth is, they're glorified caretakers and tax gatherers. As long as they pay their dues and keep things in order they can do what they like with their shrine. It's worth coming all the way from Caesarea just to remind them how powerless they are. 'What are you charging this man with? Why don't you deal with him yourselves?' I love to hear them tell me that they can't put anyone to death, because we don't allow it. That's our prerogative. There is no king but Caesar.

Here's the prisoner. It looks like they've been kind to him so far – a few bruises to his face, that's all. Let me see what I can get out of him. 'Why are you here? What have you done? Are you by any chance "king of the Jews?"' He's smart all right. He knows how not to give a straight answer. He should be a politician. But I have to say, he doesn't look the part. And if his followers ran off when he was taken, they couldn't have had much faith in their king, could they? He's no messiah. He talks too much about truth and getting his authority from some other world to lead a rebellion. I'm inclined to give him a beating and let him go.

Oh dear, the priests and the Pharisees don't like my suggestion. They're asking for somebody called Barabbas to be swapped for Jesus. He must be one of the bandits we've got locked up. My first thought is that he could cause trouble, but I'm told he was acting alone. So maybe not. It's getting rather noisy out there. Especially now that I've dressed their Jesus up like a king and presented him to them. 'Look, Judeans, here is your king.' What a pathetic figure he is. They still want me to crucify him. Maybe. Maybe not.

Now they say he's guilty of blasphemy. 'He claims to be the Son of God.' Oh, really? I'm not ready for this. 'King of the Jews' I can manage. 'Son of God' – that's straying onto Caesar's pitch. What am I not being told about this man? I ask him where he's from and he refuses to answer. He tells me I have no real power over him. Only what his god allows. This is getting too hot. I should refuse to give in to their demands and release him. He's not going to cause any trouble, is he? But on the other hand, if I do let him go, who is he really? Surely he couldn't possibly be a threat to Caesar, could he?

No way am I going to let these noisy Jews have the last word. I'll give them all something to think about. Let me see what happens when I taunt them some more. 'Here's your son-of-a-god king. Think what a king like this can do for you. Do you really want me to crucify your son-of-a-god king?' They're quicker off the mark than I expect. 'We have no king but Caesar.' That's what I want to hear these chief priests say. Of course you have no king but Caesar. It's Caesar who takes your taxes. Caesar whose soldiers march through your streets. Caesar who appoints your high priests. 'We have no king but Caesar.' Music to my ears. There is no king but Caesar. We're agreed on that. You want this man crucified? That's fine by me. You've just used him to heap shame on yourselves.

I tell the centurion to make sure the charge says 'king of the Jews' in every language these people understand. I want to rub their faces in the dirt of Golgotha. This pathetic, strung-up Jew is as close as anyone gets to ruling the world where Caesar is king. And don't you ever forget it.

How John uses the story of Pilate

John uses the story of Jesus before the Jewish and Roman authorities to explore deeper issues of authority and power. Where Jerusalem is concerned, these have been surfacing in the narrative since chapter 5. The Jewish leaders have had ample opportunity to pass judgement on Jesus because, as he reminded Annas after his arrest, he had said nothing in secret but had always put his teaching in the public realm. What made Jesus particularly dangerous in their eyes was his popularity. A subversive who drew crowds could not be tolerated, and could only be dealt with effectively by a combination of Jewish and Roman power. Hence the Sanhedrin's desire to draw Pilate into their power games.

John's account of Jesus' conflict with the Jewish leaders probes the source of their authority. He uses what he sees as Jesus' unambiguous heavenly authority as a mirror in which to view theirs. By the time Jesus is arrested, John has left his audience in no doubt about what he wishes to reflect back to them. This is not the case with Roman authority. What Pilate represents has been present throughout the Gospel, but only as the assumed yet unacknowledged backdrop. Jesus' arrest and his rapid dispatch to Pilate's residence provide the opportunity to turn the spotlight on Rome.

The synoptic Gospels may give the impression that Jerusalem is really in the driving seat and that Rome's representative is weak and vacillating. John sheds fresh light, and confirms the picture of the Pilate we know from Jewish sources. He is quick to expose the powerlessness of the Jerusalem authorities when they present Jesus to him as a criminal, in his 'take him yourselves and judge him according to your own law'. He knows that this is not part of the deal Rome has struck with them. John has them admit as much: 'We are not permitted to put anyone to death', a statement which incidentally also confirms Jesus' authority over them, because he had earlier spoken of dying by being 'lifted up' rather than stoned (12:32). Likewise, Pilate's declaration of Jesus' innocence says more about Rome's rule over Jerusalem than his sympathy towards Jesus. 'I find no case against him' is as good as telling the Jewish leaders that they will have to try harder if they want to wring any favours from him.

Jesus' silence before Pilate in the synoptic Gospels is a source of amazement to him, and a sign of Jesus' strength and authority, even when he is at his most vulnerable. John is not content with this silence, however, and spells out the nature of what is implicit in the synoptics. Pilate is not really interested in whether Jesus is king of the Jews until he reveals the source of his authority. For John, this is always heavenly, from above. So he has Jesus tell Pilate that his kingdom is 'not of this world'. Like much of John's dualistic language this is often misunderstood, as if Jesus were the head of a spiritual, otherworldly realm that stands above the manoeuvrings of this world's politics.

Nothing could be further from the truth. Throughout his ministry Jesus has challenged the politics of Jerusalem: the power of its leaders to order life according to their reading of the law, and their privileged place in a world that to all intents and purposes belongs to Rome. Now before Pilate he has the chance to call Rome to account.

He tells Caesar's representative that he is from the realm of truth, something that the governor cannot comprehend. His 'what is truth?' reminds John's audience of what they have known from the beginning. As Sophia-Logos incarnate, Jesus is God's true light, who comes into the world full of God's grace and truth. He is not just a witness to truth, but the truth itself, the true and living way to the Father, the true vine that is God's people Israel, truly human in the way he lives for God and from God. Those whose lives are shaped and directed by his word are true disciples, who know the truth that frees them from the world's slavery to sin. Truth's nemesis is the devil, the father of lies, a murderer from the beginning. If Jesus is the embodiment and measure of God's truth, truth can only be life-giving, and sin life-denying in the broadest sense imaginable.

We get the impression that all this would be beyond Pilate if he took the trouble to enquire further. As it is, he can only mock what he does not understand. The ritual degradation of Jesus' honour is carried out in this Gospel in the middle of Pilate's interrogation, not at the end as it is in Matthew and Mark. The soldiers' 'Hail, King of the Jews' is a cruel parody of the way Jesus has been greeted elsewhere in the Gospel. It is as if Rome can only deal with one who challenges the basis of its authority through violence and humiliation. Pilate takes his victim outside to display him to the Jewish leaders, only to use him to remind them once again of their impotence. 'Behold the man. Take him yourselves and crucify him.'

The Jewish leaders are not finished yet, and they find one more way of engaging Pilate's attention. The reason they want to be rid of Jesus – blasphemy – should be of real concern to Pilate, because 'he has claimed to be the Son of God'. Pilate sees this as Jesus stepping into Caesar's shoes. He is now at his most disturbed, and he raises the issue at the heart of Jesus' ongoing disputes with his enemies in Jerusalem: 'where are you from?' (7:25-30; 8:14-23). Only now is Jesus silent, in a show of strength that defies Pilate's presumed power over him. He breaks his silence to remind Pilate that whatever power he uses against him is on loan to him from above. The same is true of the Jewish leaders waiting outside. Rome and Jerusalem have colluded in bringing Jesus to this moment. But Jesus' own people are guilty of the greater sin because they refuse to listen to the God whose truth they claim to know, preferring instead the father of lies and his death-dealing ways.

Pilate reaches the point where he is not prepared to allow the Jew in front of him and the Jews outside any further say. But his desire to release Jesus is blocked by the Jews, who call into question his loyalty to Caesar. There is only one way for him to prove them wrong, but not at the expense of acceding to their wishes. So he brings Jesus – presumably still dressed in royal regalia – out to them again, and sits him on the judgement seat outside the praetorium. 'Here is your king,' he says sarcastically and mockingly. This time he uses Jesus to draw out of them the ultimate blasphemy: 'we have no king but the emperor' – who, as they know only too well, is happy to call himself God's son. What more could Pilate ask for? He gives nothing away in letting them have what they want. On the contrary, they play into his hands. On the cusp of Passover, as they prepare to celebrate their longing to be free, they acknowledge that they are slaves to the rule he represents.

Victory to Rome, then, won with the help of a troublesome Galilean rabbi and the minimum bloodshed at this volatile festival. Now all that remains is to make the Jewish leaders' defeat as public as possible. Pilate insists on having the last word on the inscription fastened to the cross. 'Jesus of Nazareth, the king of the Jews' gives the prisoner's name and the reason for his execution, written in three languages for all the world to know. As if to say, 'this is the best the Jews can manage – just remember who is the real king of the Jews'.

John has developed the story of Jesus' appearances before Judea's Jewish and Roman rulers into a critique of political power. Like the high priest he despises, his Pilate is also capable of the most profound irony. Sitting Jesus on the judgement seat, enthroning him on the cross as the King of the Jews, only serves to demonstrate what it means to have a kingdom that is 'not from this world'. Caiaphas and Pilate rule by manipulation and deceit, hypocrisy and violence. If this is how the kingdoms that are 'of this world' operate, little wonder that Jesus made himself scarce when a Galilean crowd wanted to make him king (6:15). On his way to be crucified, Jesus calls into question the versions of worldly authority and power played out in Jerusalem and Rome. The life-giving truth he embodies in all that takes him to the cross is the ultimate criterion of God's wise ways for his world. In John's eyes, anything less is lies, deception and death.

Reflections

Jesus' silence before Pilate in John's Gospel is not as evident as it is in the others. Yet there is enough to make an impression on Pilate. Or perhaps John is suggesting that there is more to silence than saying nothing. Silence symbolises the refusal to engage with another, to play by their rules.

Silence is of course ambiguous. The right to be silent when questioned by police can protect a person from intimidation. But 'silent treatment' in a relationship can be a form of bullying. By refusing to answer Pilate, Jesus is neither protective nor intimidating. He is acting out the role of God's servant in Isaiah 53:7, whose silence before his oppressors is a sign of his loyalty to the higher authority he serves.

Jesus' silence signals that he is answerable not to Rome or Jerusalem, but to an authority 'not of this world' that governs everything he says and does. Paradoxically, keeping silent denies these earthly rulers the last word. What power they have over him, and anyone else for that matter, is delegated rather than earned.

Where do you think it is appropriate to practise the silence of Jesus in the world you know? What more is there to this silence than simply saying nothing? What maintains its force as testimony to higher authority, and prevents it from becoming manipulative or abusive?

SIXTEEN

Joseph of Arimathea
John 19:38-42

Background

All four Gospels have Jesus' body buried by Joseph of Arimathea, who appears in their narratives for this sole purpose and then disappears without trace.[53] Though the accounts are broadly similar, there are some differences. Mark describes him as a respected member of the Jewish ruling council who was looking for the kingdom of God. He is courageous enough to ask Pilate to release Jesus' body for burial, which happens once his death has been confirmed by a centurion. Joseph wraps Jesus' body in a linen shroud and lays it in a rock-hewn tomb, which he then seals by rolling a stone against the entrance. It is not clear whether Mark sees Joseph as a disciple of Jesus. He may simply have been a pious Jew who did not want the land to be defiled by an unburied corpse, particularly on the eve of a Passover-tide Sabbath.

Matthew says nothing of Joseph's membership of the council. He has him as a disciple of Jesus who is wealthy enough to have his own tomb in Jerusalem, despite living away from the city in Arimathea (the location of which is now unknown). Matthew mentions the newness of the tomb to indicate that Jesus' was the only body it contained. So when it was later found empty, the only explanation could be that something must have happened to it. Luke retains Mark's ambiguity about Joseph. He highlights Joseph's traditional piety, which provided good grounds for his actions, and also that he dissented from the Sanhedrin's decision to have Jesus arrested and sent to Pilate to be crucified. Like Matthew, he has Jesus buried in a new tomb, though without mentioning whether it actually belonged to Joseph.

John develops Joseph's character further, as he does with others we know from the synoptic Gospels. His Joseph is a secret disciple rather than a member of the ruling council. He is afraid of Jewish opposition to Jesus, which puts him with Nicodemus. Not surprisingly, then, the two of them come together to bury Jesus, in a new garden tomb near to where he was crucified. Only John has Jesus' body anointed as he is buried, with a largesse of spices. The burial clothes too are more than the other Gospels describe. In the words of one writer, Jesus is given 'a burial that befits a king'.[54]

---

53. Matthew 27:57-61; Mark 15:42-47; Luke 23:50-56; John 19:38-42.
54. David Allen, 'Secret Disciples. Nicodemus and Joseph of Arimathea', in Chris Keith and Larry Hurtado (eds.), *Jesus among Friends and Enemies. A Historical and Literary Introduction to Jesus in the Gospels*, Grand Rapids: Baker Academic, 2011, p. 168.

Doubts as to whether Joseph was a historical figure hang on the plausibility of his actions. The bodies of crucified men were not generally given an honourable burial. Some have wondered whether a respected and influential member of the Jewish council would have gone to so much trouble to take care of the body of Jesus personally, and then disappear without trace from the earliest Christian records outside the Gospels. But Josephus and Philo report similar burials, as does the apocryphal book of Tobit, who regularly buried the dead bodies of his people as an act of piety.[55]

Joseph resurfaces in writings from the second, sixth and twelfth centuries, which expand and in some cases alter the evangelists' accounts, and in the Glastonbury legends, in which he is said to have buried the Holy Grail (the cup containing Jesus' blood) at the foot of Glastonbury Tor.

Though Joseph only appears in John's Gospel after Jesus has died, I imagine him witnessing the crucifixion and reflecting on his struggle to overcome the fear that forced him to keep his loyalty to Jesus a secret.

Joseph's story

I wanted no part in what happened to Jesus. I never denied that Jesus made all of us feel uncomfortable. Especially when he sat so loosely to our laws at times, and challenged us about whether we were doing right by using them to preserve our special place in the world. Didn't the prophets say that justice and mercy and humility and looking after the poor are the most important ways of showing our devotion to God? I wasn't the only member of our synagogue community who felt there was more to Jesus than some untrained upstart of a Galilean rabbi, whose over-active ego was an attempt to compensate for his dubious parentage. It's just that none of us who wanted to give him a hearing had the courage to stand up for what we thought. We were afraid of those with the loudest voices. We let ourselves be silenced all too often.

Something in me stirred, though, when I heard that the leaders of my own people confessed to Pilate that Caesar is our king. I thought: 'is this the price we have to pay to hold onto our inheritance as God's people?' Couldn't they see that Pilate was using their desire to get rid of Jesus to make fools of them? He was just playing with them, like he was with Jesus. 'We have no king but Caesar' is much more blasphemous than anything Jesus ever said. At least he was defending his right to heal the sick and care for the poor in the name of our God. But our leaders were confessing their faith in a world governed by force and fear.

I followed as Jesus was taken from Pilate's residence to the outskirts of the city. Skull Hill is where the Romans execute their prisoners. It's like a sport to them, a ritual of humiliation, torture and a long, drawn-out death. Particularly at this time of year when they like to remind

---

55. Tobit 1:16-20.

us who's really in charge. It gives such a hollow ring to our Passover celebrations. Freedom? Will we ever be free as long as Rome rules over us – as long as our leaders are more concerned about holding onto their privilege and power? Not that we have any real power, it's just more convenient for Rome to use our own people to govern us. I was scared of standing up to them, like the rest of us who felt some sympathy for Jesus. I wasn't strong enough to speak up openly for him. Only to follow at a safe distance, pretending to be a spectator like the rest.

I saw him being strung up with bandits. If it wasn't so tragic, it would have been comical. How could you rank him with people who see the sword as the way to win our freedom? And still Pilate was playing with us. It was as if 'we have no king but Caesar' was echoing in his ears. 'The King of the Jews' was the charge written over Jesus, as if Pilate was saying: 'This is as near to a royal throne as any Jew will ever get while I'm governor of this province. Don't you dare forget it.' His soldiers did what soldiers are paid to do. They stripped the last vestiges of dignity from their prisoners, and divided the spoils among themselves. All except Jesus' tunic. They threw dice for that. I wasn't sure why at the time. Did they see something other than a condemned Jew hanging there? Did they think he was worthy of at least some respect – even if only for his clothing?

Who would have thought there could be anything but brutality and grief in such a god-forsaken place? But there was a dying man – he could barely breathe – speaking to his only followers with the courage to come so close. A group of women – one was his mother. And his closest disciple. I wondered whether it was too soon for them to be thinking what their lives would be like without him. He used what must have been his last breath to answer my question. 'He's your son now. She's your mother.' Who would have thought such tenderness or humanity could sound out in a place like that? It wasn't quite his last breath. 'I'm thirsty,' he said, but he got nothing more than sour wine. Then, suddenly, it really was his last breath. 'It is finished.'

Almost. One more act of brutality. Our leaders wanted the victims' legs breaking to make sure they were dead before sundown and the start of Passover and the Sabbath. Then their bodies could be taken down. 'We must make sure we don't offend the law of Moses.' Could they not hear their own hypocrisy? 'We have no king but Caesar – but let's make sure we keep our God's laws.' At least Jesus was spared. He was already dead – but just to make sure, a soldier stuck a spear in his side. It must have ripped open his lungs because out came blood and water. He'll never breathe again.

Something stirred in me, though. I didn't have the courage to speak up for him when he was alive. But I did find the strength to go with my friend Nicodemus, a member of our ruling council who had wanted to give Jesus a fair hearing, to ask Pilate if we could bury him with the respect due to a true son of Abraham. I remember my conversation with Nicodemus as we went home after sealing the tomb: 'Why have we been more open in our devotion to him since he died than ever we were when he was alive?' And his reply: 'Maybe it's as much as we can manage for now. Who knows what tomorrow may bring – for all of us?'

How John uses Joseph's story

John does not suggest that Joseph of Arimathea was there at the cross, or that he contributed anything to the way he understands the crucifixion. But as one of those in this Gospel who gave such personal attention to the dead body of Jesus – presumably at some financial cost, and risk to his own reputation and safety – Joseph invites us to look carefully at the one who was crucified and the way John pictures his execution.

Though the accounts of Jesus' death in all four Gospels have a lot in common, each has its own distinctive features. John leaves out a number of details found in the synoptic Gospels. There is no Simon of Cyrene to carry the cross beam of a man exhausted by a series of overnight interrogations, accusations, mockery and beatings. Here Jesus carries his own cross to signify his authority and strength, something he spoke of earlier in the Gospel when he said of the good shepherd, 'No-one takes my life from me. I lay it down of my own accord' (10:18). John has no barrage of mockery for Jesus to endure, either from the general public, the Jewish rulers, the duty soldiers or the others crucified with him. There is no taunting at his inability to save himself. Neither is there darkness between the sixth and ninth hours, or the tearing of the temple curtain, details that in the other Gospels associate the death of Jesus with the prophetic visions of the end of the present age and the coming of the time of salvation. Heavenly signs and critical bystanders come earlier in the Gospel, when Jesus speaks about this 'hour'. They are there in the thunder that he hears as the reassuring voice of his Father, and the questions of a crowd that cannot believe in a messiah who has to die (12:27-36).

John's account of the inscription on the cross is much richer than the other Gospels. The words that Pilate insists on posting are designed to ridicule Jesus and humiliate his people. Who would think that this pathetic figure from Nazareth of all places (1:46) might be a king to compare with Israel's true king, Caesar? Words in three languages, repeated for the sake of the chief priests, gather up the responses of those more sympathetic to Jesus at the beginning and end of his public ministry, from Nathanael's 'you are the king of Israel' in 1:49 to the pilgrim crowd's 'Hosanna! Blessed is the one who comes in the name of the Lord – the King of Israel!' in 12:13. Jesus managed to escape from those who wanted to crown him in Galilee, because the hopes he excited in them were very much 'of this world'. On the unpromising soil of Golgotha, he is willing to be enthroned at the heart of a kingdom that is ordered by the truth he has lived to the end.

Soldiers were used to dividing up the property of their defeated victims – the spoils of war, and here the clothing of those they have executed. Only John mentions Jesus' tunic, an undergarment made from a single piece of cloth. It is left intact, and the four soldiers cast lots for it. Like the other evangelists, John sees Scripture being fulfilled, quoting Psalm 22:18 and alluding perhaps to Aaron's priestly ephod in Exodus 28:32, also made not to be torn. Does John see Jesus' undivided tunic as an anticipation of the temple of his body that he promised to raise up in three days – a temple in the most ungodly place, outside the holy city? (2:19-22). There are other signs of this renewed temple taking shape as Jesus is crucified. The water that flows from his side when the soldier stabs it with his spear to make sure he is dead fulfils his promise of the rivers of living water that flow from his heart, symbolised by the water that was carried from the pool of Siloam into the temple at the feast of Booths (7:37-39).[56] Living water is what he also promised to the Samaritan woman, when he spoke of true worshippers meeting God not in temples or on holy mountains but 'in Spirit and truth' (4:7-26).

Jesus' body-as-temple is a hospitable place for the birth of a community of true worshippers. Where the other Gospels have women watching Jesus die from a distance, John has them standing by the cross, close enough to hear his dying words (19:25-27). What he says to his mother and the disciple he loves (already united by their anonymity) creates a new family, in which the traditional ties of flesh and blood are transcended by the bonds of faith and love. On this new holy ground, women stand alongside men. One of them, Mary Magdalene, will soon become the first apostle of the new temple community (20:18).

All this is happening at Passover-tide. In this Gospel Jesus is crucified as the Passover lambs are being slaughtered, beginning at noon on the day of Preparation (19:14). His ministry began with John the Baptiser bearing witness to the Lamb of God who takes away the sin of the world. It reaches its glorious end as the same Lamb of God finishes his work.[57] To show that this is not just a coincidence of timing, John adds further scriptural touches. The thirsty Jesus is given sour wine to drink on a sponge at the end of a hyssop branch. His thirst alludes to Psalm 69:21, but the hyssop branch goes back to Exodus 12:22, where hyssop is dipped in Passover lambs' blood and used to smear it on doorposts and lintels as a mark of the freedom to come. At the very end, once Jesus is dead, his legs are left unbroken by the soldiers who are ordered to hasten the deaths of their crucified charges. The resonating scriptures are again from the Passover story, where the bones of Passover lambs are never broken.[58]

---

56. John connects the piercing itself with Zechariah 12:10, which belongs with the prophet's promise of the renewal of Jerusalem and its temple, when living waters will flow out from Jerusalem (Zechariah 14:8).

57. Jesus' last words in this Gospel are not a cry of forsakenness (Matthew and Mark) or trust (Luke), but triumph: 'It is finished' (19:30; see 17:4).

58. John 19:36; see Exodus 12:46; Numbers 9:12.

A temple not made with hands, a kingdom not of this world, a king reigning from the most unlikely throne, the Lamb of God slaughtered on a gibbet. The true holy place, where the glory of God dwells in a community drawn from the whole world, represented here by women and men and elsewhere in John's story by Jews, Greeks and Samaritans, gathered into one flock and marked for freedom by the unceasing prayer that is the freely given life of Jesus. None of this would have been apparent at the time. Early in the narrative, John indicated that the full significance of Jesus would only dawn on his followers later. Only when he had been raised from the dead (2:22, 12:16) and the Spirit had come (14:26) would they truly see. The evangelist leaves the impression that his witness is the fruit of deep reflection and sustained prayer. But his message is anything but otherworldly. The power that flows from this holy ground is about to make the whole world new.

Reflections

None of the evangelists dwells on the details of Jesus' crucifixion. It was hardly necessary. Their audiences were familiar enough with the brutality and humiliation of public execution. They are more interested in drawing out the meaning of what was to many in their world a genuine obstacle to faith in Jesus as God's anointed one (1 Corinthians 1:23). One of John's great gifts is as an artist. In a Gospel that is very much about seeing, he uses words to paint pictures that appeal to the heart as well as the mind. His depiction of Jesus' crucifixion is one of his finest and most moving.

The cross as a religious symbol is ambiguous. What are we to make of the often resigned expression on the face of the figure on the crucifix? Or the polished wood of a cross from which Jesus is absent? Or the jewel-encrusted processional cross leading dignitaries into and out of a cathedral's worship? Or the cross on a crusader's uniform? Or the 18-carat gold cross worn around the neck?

As an artist, John is at home with ambiguity. It leaves room for others to respond to what he offers. His images of the cross gather up the story of a man who might otherwise have been stoned to death. Jesus' cross was an instrument of oppression and torture, inflicted on one who was judged too dangerous to live freely, one of the compromises necessary to maintain the imperial peace. All this and more, says John. The cross of Jesus is where heaven and earth meet. Its very ignominy is its glory.

Let the attention given by Joseph of Arimathea to the crucified body of Jesus draw you to the pictures John paints of what Jesus' death means for him and his audience. Which of his images are you particularly drawn to, and which do you find most challenging or difficult? Where do you see the ignominy and glory of Jesus' crucifixion reflected in the world you know? How does John's symbolism of the cross inspire the way you live out your faith?

SEVENTEEN

Mary Magdalene
John 19:25-27; 20:1-18

Background

Mary is called after her village, Magdala, a fish-processing centre on the western shore of the Sea of Galilee, south of Capernaum. She is nearly always mentioned first in the evangelists' lists of Jesus' female disciples. She is named 12 times, more than most of Jesus' male apostles. Only Luke mentions her in the main body of his Gospel. She is one of Jesus' female disciples in Luke 8:2, 3, where she is linked with women who had experienced illness and distress, as well as having the means to support an itinerant rabbi and his followers. Luke's note that 'seven demons had gone out from her' suggests that she had a history of mental health problems. A rabbi whose followers included women of independent means, some with reputations of challenging behaviour, would have attracted suspicion and even disapproval in some quarters.

In the Gospels of Matthew and Mark, Mary is named as one of the women who have come with Jesus from Galilee, and now watch him die from a distance. Luke does not name her at this point in his account, though he later implies that she was there.[59] What is also important is that Mary and the other women see where Jesus is buried. They provide the connecting thread of witness to his death, burial and what follows, because they and not the male disciples are the first visitors to the tomb of Jesus early on the first day of the week.[60] In Mark and Luke, they intend to anoint Jesus' body, and in Matthew simply to see the tomb. The presence of women as witnesses is not something anyone at the time would have invented, given the low status of women and the assumption that their evidence could not be trusted. It is not surprising that Jesus' male disciples regard their report of what they encountered at the tomb as 'an idle tale'.

Mary appears for the first time in John's Gospel in 19:25, by Jesus' cross with his mother, two other women and the Beloved Disciple. John says nothing about her seeing where Jesus is buried. She visits his garden tomb early on the first day of the week, with no intention to anoint Jesus' body because Joseph of Arimathea and Nicodemus have already done that. Is she alone (she later tells Peter that 'we do not know where they have laid Jesus'), or has John reduced the other Gospels' group of women to one? Only John includes the account of her meeting Jesus by the tomb

---

59. Matthew 27:55, 56, 61; Mark 15:40, 41, 47; Luke 23:49, 55; Luke 24:10.
60. Matthew 28:1-8; Mark 16:1-8; Luke 24:1-12.

(20:1-18). Some of the details are typically Johannine: the desire to touch Jesus (as with Thomas later, in 20:25); his reference to ascending to the Father, and opening up his relationship with 'my Father . . . my God' to others. There are also links with Luke. Mary's not recognising Jesus at first reminds us of the disciples walking back to Emmaus (Luke 24:13-35). She eventually realises who is speaking to her when Jesus says something familiar, just like the disciples in Emmaus when Jesus says grace over the meal they share. Mary's assumption that Jesus' body has been stolen is only found in John, as is his description of her as the first apostle of the resurrection, though this is implied in the other Gospels. The value John places on her witness is in stark contrast to Paul, who makes no reference to Jesus' resurrection appearances to women in 1 Corinthians 15:5-8.

Mary's story has a considerable afterlife in Christian iconography and mythology. The accounts of her in the Gospels contribute to what has been called 'the composite Mary' of Christian devotion, a figure that combines elements of a number of Gospel women, including the anonymous prostitute who wipes Jesus' feet with her hair and Mary the sister of Martha.[61] Some of the apocryphal Gospels written in the second and third Christian centuries regard Mary Magdalene as Jesus' favourite disciple, with a deeper understanding of his teachings than the male disciples. In Western Christianity she features both as a penitent sinner and a symbol of the contemplative life. William Blake re-introduced her to English literature as a prostitute, and the noun 'Magdalene' came to mean 'penitent prostitute'. More recently Mary features strongly in the musicals *Jesus Christ Superstar* and *Godspell*, where she is almost as important as Jesus. She is a symbol of erotic temptation in Nikos Kazantzakis' *The Last Temptation of Christ*, and in Dan Brown's *The Da Vinci Code* she is Jesus' wife and successor, the archetype of the so-called 'sacred feminine'.

I imagine Mary reflecting on her closeness to Jesus, and what she sees of him on Golgotha and in the garden by his tomb.

Mary Magdalene's story

I've never been so close to a crucifixion.
Close enough to touch.
I couldn't have kept my distance.
Not the way he was,
always ready to touch when it was needed.
Even at the end he used his last breath
to give his mother a new son.
He couldn't move his arms.
No way could he touch.
But somehow he still managed to reach them.
To hold all of us.

---

61. Luke 7:36-50; 10:38-42; John 11:1-44; 12:1-7.

Peter told me where his body was laid, when it was getting dark, before the Sabbath started. Joseph and Nicodemus. I'd seen them once or twice. I could never work them out. But they were brave enough to ask the Governor for his body, so they could give him a decent burial. I saw the new tomb, the garden. His body wrapped in linen and spices. So many spices. No fond farewell.

I went back to the lodging house we rented for Passover. I decided to stay there until after the Sabbath. Then I'd go back to the tomb and say my own goodbye. I couldn't sleep that first night. Or the second. It didn't seem to matter whether it was day or night, I just drifted in and out of sleep. And all the time my dreams were shaking what little sleep I had out of me.

So restless I had to get up
with the sun
the day after Sabbath.
Get dressed.
Keep quiet.
No sense waking anyone.
Go out by myself.
The pull of the tomb stronger now
than sleep.
Wanting to be where
I knew he was.

I told myself that wouldn't be possible because of the big stone Peter said they'd put across the entrance. But I thought if I could stand by the stone for a while, he'd only be on the other side. I could talk to him. Say goodbye.

It's not right.
Something's happened.
It wasn't like that
two days ago when I left it.
It's been opened up.

Had I come to the right place? I was sure I had. A garden with a tomb. How many gardens with tombs are there so near to where he was crucified? I got close enough to see that his body wasn't there. I ran back to the house as fast as I could. By the time I got there I was frantic. I woke Peter up and told him what I'd seen. 'You're dreaming, woman,' he said, as he got one of the others and made for the tomb. I couldn't keep up with them. They passed me going the other way, back to the lodgings. 'Empty,' they said. 'Nothing there. The body's gone. We'll wake the others.'

So I wasn't dreaming, I said to myself as the tomb tugged at me again. Why did I have to look inside after what Peter said? But he was wrong. This time the tomb wasn't empty. There were two men dressed in white, like they were wearing the grave clothes. I thought they were playing a horrible trick. I was in floods of tears, and they asked me some stupid question about why I was weeping. 'Tell me what's happened to the body.' I shouted at them. I couldn't help myself. 'I just want to know where he is.'

There was someone outside, in the garden near the tomb. I couldn't see properly, the light was too dim. Was it the man who looks after the garden? So early in the morning? I shouted at him too. 'Tell me where you've taken him. I just want to know where my Jesus is.'

> And then I heard my name.
> The stranger in the garden by the tomb called me
> by my name.
> Mary ...
> Was I hearing things?
> Was my mind playing tricks again
> like the old days?
> Mary ...
> Only one man I know says
> my name like that
> and the last time I saw him he was hanging
> on a cross over there.
> And now he's gone.
> Dead. Gone.
> Mary ...
> Is it? Are you?
> My rabbi? Jesus?
> Jesus!

And then my arms took over. I reached for him like I always did. I had to hold him to make sure I wasn't dreaming. I remember thinking I'd wake up any moment, like I had so many times the last two nights, numbed by his absence. But I didn't wake up. I wasn't dreaming.

> He wouldn't let me hold onto him.
> 'Go and tell the others.'
> I ran as fast as I could.
> No – faster.
> I didn't turn round.
> I didn't look back.
> I just ran to the house and screamed
> at Peter and the others:
> 'I've seen the Lord!'
> Jesus! It was Jesus!
> He knew my name.
> He called me Mary.
> 'I've seen the Lord!'

I collapsed in a heap, in floods of tears, no more words. Any minute now I'll wake up, I thought. But I didn't. And I haven't. I wasn't dreaming.

I HAVE SEEN THE LORD!

How John uses the story of Mary Magdalene

Of all those who may have visited Jesus' tomb in the early morning, John focuses on Mary Magdalene, and presents her as a model of true discipleship. Unlike most of the male disciples, she is faithful to Jesus to the very end. By standing with him at the cross and visiting his tomb, she reveals her determination to be where his body is.

The question Jesus puts to her in the garden, 'For whom are you looking?', is similar to the one he asked the two disciples of John the Baptiser on the third day of the Gospel's narrative (1:38). One of them also calls Jesus 'rabbi', as Mary does here when she recognises him. Up to this point Mary is looking for the dead body of Jesus. The man she meets by the tomb is no more than a gardener at first. But when she hears him call her by name, she realises who he is. John's audience will recognise this as the voice of the Good Shepherd, who knows his own sheep by name (10:3-5, 14, 15) and calls Mary, like Lazarus, to exchange the world of death for the realm of eternal life.

John shows her growing appreciation of the one who calls her name. The gardener becomes 'rabbouni', though Mary thinks she can still cling to him as she used to. But a new kind of relationship is opening up, one that depends on the soon-to-come Spirit released by Jesus' return to his Father. Mary has already glimpsed this when she stood by the cross and heard Jesus calling his mother and the disciple he loves into a discipleship that is family-like: 'woman, behold your son; behold your mother'. Disciples who once were his servants and friends (15:15) are now his 'brothers' (and presumably sisters too, in view of the prominence of women among them), and his Father is their Father too. By the time she reaches them, her rabbouni has become her 'Lord', and she is the first apostle of his resurrection.

Mary is not only a model disciple but also a faithful and trustworthy witness. In the other Gospels too, the story told by the women who visited Jesus' tomb early on the first day of the week turned out to be foundational in the Jesus movement. Typically, John makes more of what we know from elsewhere. Mary tells her brother disciples that she has 'seen the Lord'. They repeat what she tells them to Thomas, and he eventually makes it his own. It is as if the evangelist draws a clear line that connects the witness of Mary, the other disciples, Thomas and those who in his own day and beyond who are blessed because they believe without seeing (20:18, 24-29). The faith of later disciples rests on the testimony of Mary. To see her as a trustworthy witness is a high accolade from John, for whom the testimony of the Beloved Disciple is paramount. This woman's story, says the evangelist, is worth knowing.

It is the foundation of a gospel that breaks new ground by crossing all kinds of boundaries within and around Israel.

Reflections

As a model disciple and primary witness, Mary has a developing faith, like that of other witnesses in this Gospel. Think back to the stories of Nathanael, the Samaritan woman, the man born blind, Martha and Mary, with Thomas still to come. John certainly compresses the way faith grows in these examples, but this is because he wants to demonstrate that what we might call the DNA of faith is present from their very first meetings with Jesus.

Two things come across clearly in all their stories. The first is the way faith in Jesus uses everyday experiences as its raw material. So we see something of a community celebrating a wedding, the daily work of the Samaritan woman and the constraints imposed by her culture, the hunger of Galilean peasants and their vulnerability to rising food prices, the paralysed man's disability and the poverty and prejudice he experiences, the bullying and hostility endured by the blind man, the bereavement and disappointment of Mary and Martha, the questioning and doubt of Thomas.

The second is the way these mundane experiences open people up to faith in Jesus. John's line of witnesses begin by seeing Jesus as a human being rather than the incarnation of God's Sophia-Logos: a rabbi from Nazareth, a guest at a wedding, a tired Jewish man, a traditional healer, the closest of friends, a trusted yet puzzling companion, a man in a garden. Only by bringing their experiences of everyday life into dialogue with the one who occupies the same ground as them can John's witnesses hope to see Jesus as the human face of God, the one Mary calls 'Lord'.

Use the stories of Mary and her brother and sister disciples to reflect on the way your faith develops and the direction it is taking. Which of your everyday experiences bring you closest to the ordinary humanity of Jesus? How does the common ground you and he occupy allow the DNA of your faith to grow? What direction is your witness taking as a person of faith in a family of disciples?

EIGHTEEN

Thomas

John 11:1-16; 14:1-6; 20:24-29

Background

Thomas appears in all four lists of the twelve disciples,[62] but this is the extent of his presence in the synoptic Gospels and the Acts of the Apostles. By contrast he has an important role in John's Gospel. On all but one occasion (14:5) he is introduced as 'Thomas, who was called the Twin', as if to distinguish him from another Thomas, known perhaps to the evangelist and his community.

Thomas is remembered for his doubts about the resurrection of Jesus, but there is more to the character John outlines. Thomas is sceptical rather than uncertain. He asks awkward questions about the faith of others, and John uses this to draw out the meaning of belief and discipleship. In 11:1-16, Thomas appears in the fog of confusion and misunderstanding generated by Jesus' response to the news of his beloved friend Lazarus' illness. Jesus changes his mind about leaving the safety of his refuge across the Jordan and travelling to Bethany in Judea, where he will doubtless attract the attention of his enemies. The disciples' failure to understand his talk of Lazarus' death as 'sleep' forces him to abandon metaphor in favour of plain speech. His decision to go to Bethany provokes Thomas' ironic aside that reflects John's understanding of discipleship: 'Let us also go, that we may die with him.'

Thomas next appears in 14:1-6 at the Passover-tide meal, when Jesus speaks of his death as both a going from and a coming to his disciples. His attempt to reassure them that his leaving will actually benefit them falls on deaf ears. Thomas confesses his ignorance about where Jesus is going, and how he might follow him along the way. His heartfelt question, 'Lord, we do not know where you are going. How can we know the way?' draws out one of Jesus' most memorable sayings in this Gospel: 'I am the way, the truth and the life. No one comes to the Father except through me.'

Thomas' last speaking part is in 20:24-29 after Jesus' resurrection. His absence when Jesus appeared to his disciples on the evening of the day after the Sabbath provides the ideal opportunity for further questioning. He refuses to believe the other disciples' report that 'we have seen the Lord' without being able to confirm for himself that the one who allegedly appeared to them is the same person who was crucified. Again Thomas' scepticism leads to further exploration, this time of the basis of resurrection faith.

---

62. Matthew 10:3; Mark 3:18; Luke 6:15; Acts 1:13.

Thomas' final appearance in the Gospel is incidental. He is one of a group of disciples who spend a fruitless night fishing on the Sea of Tiberias. Jesus appears to them by the lake in the early morning, and is recognised at first by the Beloved Disciple. The main focus of the story is on Jesus' rehabilitation of Peter after he had denied being one of his followers.

Like most of the twelve disciples, Thomas fades from the New Testament's picture, though a number of later works carry his name. *The Gospel of Thomas* was probably compiled in the second century AD as a collection of 114 sayings said to be from the risen Jesus and written down by Thomas. Half of them resemble material in the Gospels and the rest have a gnostic[63] flavour. Interestingly, some scholars see the similarities between parts of John's Gospel and the Gospel of Thomas as John's attempts to refute the teachings of a rival Jesus movement. Also from the second century is *The Infancy Gospel of Thomas*, one of a number of contemporary writings that satisfy the hunger for details of Jesus' childhood. According to the third century work *The Acts of Thomas*, between AD 52 and 72 Thomas was a missionary in what is now known as the Kerala region of India, whose Mar Thoma church traces its origins to him.

I imagine Thomas looking back over his time with Jesus, recalling his confusion as Jesus' life was increasingly put at risk. The shockwaves of Jesus' execution leave him planning his return to Galilee, until reports of Jesus' appearances intervene.

Thomas' story

I can't make him out sometimes. I know the others feel the same. He confuses me. He talks in riddles. All this stuff about 12 hours of daylight and falling over rocks in the dark. Whether it's daytime or dark, if he goes anywhere near Jerusalem, he'll not be falling over rocks, he'll be lying underneath them. And that goes for the rest of us too!

Last time we went there for Dedication, he nearly caused a riot. How he managed to escape, heaven only knows. He will keep provoking the authorities with his talk of doing the Father's work. I said to him when he healed that paralysed man on the Sabbath, 'Why couldn't you have waited till sunset?' He hadn't walked for 38 years. A few more hours wouldn't have made any difference!

So I was relieved – we all were – when he said we were staying put when the message came about Lazarus. Don't get me wrong. We love

---

63. Gnosticism emerged in the second century AD as a spiritual movement influenced by elements of Christianity, Judaism, Zoroastrianism and Greek philosophy. Though Gnostic and Christian teaching differed sharply (eg in their beliefs about the goodness of the material world), there was enough overlap for gnostic beliefs to be seen as a threat to emerging Christian orthodoxy. Some gnostic teachers were drawn by the Gospel of John's presentation of Jesus as a heavenly revealer who brought salvation, though they played down the significance of his death.

Lazarus and his sisters. I hoped as much as the next man that he'd recover. But that was no time to cross into Judea. I thought we'd managed to convince him to stay here where it was safe. But two days on from hearing the news, he dragged us to Bethany. Why? He'd already told the messenger Lazarus wouldn't die. So why the hurry? Why put all our lives in danger?

'Lazarus has fallen asleep,' he said. 'I'm going to wake him up.' Well, if he'd only dropped off to sleep, he'd wake himself up. Or else Martha would – I can't imagine her letting anyone lie in bed for long.

There was no changing Jesus' mind. He was determined to cross the Jordan and put us all in danger. 'We might as well go and die with him,' I said at the time. And I wasn't joking. I think we had a narrow escape. But not for long. Raising Lazarus only provoked the authorities all the more. It made Jesus even more popular. I knew – I think we all did – it was only a matter of time before they'd come after him. And of course they did.

But not before we'd begun our celebrations of Passover. What a time that was. The weirdest Passover I've ever taken part in. Jesus always took the part of the host at the meal, but at that one he played the slave too. Kneeling at our feet, washing them. It was too much for Peter. Seeing him on the floor in front of me – in front of all of us – will stay with me forever. And then all that stuff about one of us betraying him. How to relax your friends when they're already getting more worked up by the minute! And then he talked about going away as if we'd never see him again. 'I'm going to prepare a place for you in my Father's house.' But we'd only just arrived in Jerusalem for the festival. Did he mean he wasn't coming back to Galilee with us afterwards? Where was he planning to go? To the temple? 'You know the way to the place where I'm going,' he said. No, we didn't – I told him so! How could we know the way when we didn't know the destination? 'I am the way,' he said. 'The way, the truth and the life. I'm going to my Father's house. I've no intention of leaving you behind. I'm taking you with me.' But then he talked about how we'd be hated, and the hostility we'd have to face from the synagogues, and he promised to send us a 'Spirit' that would help us, like an advocate speaking in a court room. I was baffled, I can tell you. So when they finally got him – no surprises there; praying in that little garden where we always used to gather, it was a giveaway; and Judas, what was he playing at? – when they finally got him, what were we supposed to do? I just ran, we all did. I didn't even go back to the lodgings. I stayed with some other people I knew in Jerusalem, just to keep my head down for a few days. I needed somewhere I could feel safe and work out what this was all about.

I'd made up my mind to go home, back to Galilee and fishing, once the festival was over. So after about a week I went to the lodgings to pick up my things. And I heard what I thought was the most ridiculous tale you could ever invent. The others said they'd seen

Jesus. 'What, you mean his dead body? Has it turned up then?' 'No,' they said, 'not his dead body. He's alive. He appeared to Mary by his tomb. He stood right here in this room in front of all of us. He greeted us, just like he always did: "Shalom." He showed us the wounds in his hands and his side. And he breathed the Holy Spirit on us, and told us to continue his work.'

'No,' I said, 'that's not possible.' I didn't want to hear all that. I was still reeling from the shock of his arrest and execution. 'Your minds are playing tricks. You're just seeing what you want to see. You don't want him to be dead, you want him to be still alive, just like he always was. I can't believe it. It can't have been him. The only way you'll convince me is if I get to see the wounds of a crucified man and touch him.'

They persuaded me to stay with them for a day or two, then we could all head north together. We ate a meal together that evening, like we always did. They were still going on about Jesus being alive. 'What about the tomb?' I said. 'Have you checked the tomb?' I knew they must have, but I had to ask again. They told me it was empty. 'Grave robbers,' I replied. 'Someone stole the body. And that's playing on your minds. It's making you think he's alive, because that's what you want to believe.' Just then, while we were eating and arguing, there was someone else there. I didn't notice anyone arrive, and the doors were locked as usual. 'Shalom,' he said. We just about managed to return his greeting. Then he came over to me and told me to touch the wounds in his hands and side. 'Don't doubt, Thomas, trust.'

I could hardly breathe, let alone speak. I was astounded, mystified, completely overcome. 'My Lord! My God! It is you.'

How John uses the story of Thomas

Thomas' intervention in the discussions about travelling to Lazarus and his family in Bethany is a typical piece of Johannine irony, in which characters say more than they intend. The same happens later with Caiaphas in 11:50. Following Jesus into Judea raises the level of risk to the whole group. Last time Jesus was in Jerusalem, at the feast of Dedication, his enemies tried to stone him and when that failed, they settled on seizing him. Somehow Jesus managed to evade their intentions, and found refuge and a sympathetic audience across the Jordan (10:22-42). Now the disciples are alarmed at the thought of returning to a danger zone. Thomas' remark in 11:16 has a resigned feel, but there is also a deeper meaning. Following Jesus is about dying with him, at least metaphorically. The synoptic tradition recognises this in the sayings about disciples being prepared to take up their cross (Luke underlines the metaphorical sense by adding 'daily'), and Paul sees baptism as ritualising a kind of death.[64] Thomas anticipates Jesus' words to the Greeks who want to see

---

64. Matthew 16:24; Mark 8:34; Luke 9:23; Romans 6:3; Galatians 2:19; Colossians 2:12.

him in 12:20-26, his warnings about persecution in 16:2-4 and his final conversation with Peter in 21:18, 19. John's unfolding understanding of discipleship as abiding in Christ leaves no room for what Dietrich Bonhoeffer calls 'cheap grace . . . the deadly enemy of our Church', for 'when Christ calls a man, he bids him come and die'.[65]

Thomas' next appearance brings out the connection between Jesus' parting promise of blessing and the way of the cross. At the last Passover-tide meal, after he has washed the disciples' feet as a way of modelling the call to self-sacrificing love, Jesus speaks of his going away. The disciples are alarmed by his insistence that they cannot follow him now, though later they will. Jesus sees Peter's protestation, 'Lord, why can I not follow you now? I will lay down my life for you', as bravado. When his loyalty is tested, he will be more concerned to save his own skin. Though they are often lifted from their context, Jesus' words of assurance in 14:1-6 follow his talk of costly discipleship. Thomas does not understand Jesus' talk of going away to his Father's house ahead of his followers, and his coming again to take them to himself. By now he should: 'you know the way to the place where I am going'. Again Thomas' question, 'how can we know the way?' draws out Jesus' meaning. The way to the blessing that brings peace to their troubled hearts is Jesus himself, 'the way, the truth and the life'. His going away is his return to the Father, his lifting up on the cross, the glorifying of the Son through his execution, the ascent of Jesus-Sophia. Jesus' cross is his journey. So to travel with him is to die with him, as Thomas has already pointed out without realising it. The true and life-giving way (which is how the New English Bible translates the 'I am' saying in 14:6) is to embrace his cross.

The Wisdom tradition again informs Jesus' words here. In Proverbs 1:20-33, Sophia's departure brings judgement on those who abandon her. By contrast, Jesus-Sophia's going brings God's blessing to those who keep faith with him. Wisdom's 'way' is life-giving: 'She guided [a holy people] along a marvellous way, and became a shelter to them by day, and a starry flame through the night. She brought them over the Red Sea, and led them through deep waters' (Wisdom 10:17, 18). But in the wisdom of the Jesus tradition, the way to God's salvation is always costly. Life only ever comes through the many forms of death.

Philip's subsequent and related request to Jesus opens up his remark about coming to the Father through him. This kind of travelling is what it means to know Jesus, and to know him is to know the Father who has sent him. Drawing once more on the Wisdom tradition, Jesus affirms that knowing and seeing him will open his disciples' eyes to the Father. What he says here is shot through with paradox: dying as the way to the fullness of life, for himself and for everyone. This is the sense of a saying that many find

---

65. Dietrich Bonhoeffer, *The Cost of Discipleship*, London: SCM Press, 1959, pp. 35-51, 76-83.

offensive: 'no one comes to the Father except by me'. What Jesus does not say is that 'no one knows anything about God except through me'. His positive message is that those who are prepared to travel along the costly way that is Jesus will reach its destination in his Father's house, whose hospitality is open to all.

By now the connecting threads in John's story of Thomas are becoming clearer. Following Jesus means taking risks, letting go, dying, loving. Following also means being with him, knowing him, embracing his cross, seeing the Father in him and his way. Thomas' final appearance, and the one he is most celebrated for, explores the significance of seeing (20:19-29). Thomas is missing when Jesus first appears to the whole company of disciples behind locked doors. The scene evokes the experience of John's audience, on their guard because of the local synagogue's hostility. Twice Jesus speaks the traditional Jewish greeting 'Shalom', as if to remind his followers that the gift he brings is not the world's way of peace (14:27) – imperial peace, the Pax Romana, imposed by the military power of the emperor – but its healing through the divine sacrificial love revealed in his wounds. This is nothing less than a new creation, hence Jesus' breathing the Holy Spirit over the chaos of a community devastated by his death. And to show that they have a future, he commissions them to extend his words and work, particularly the forgiveness that flows from the wounded Lamb of God who takes away the sin of the world.

And all this in the absence of Thomas, who refuses to believe his friends' report that they, like Mary Magdalene, have 'seen the Lord'. Thomas does not doubt that they have seen something or someone, only that this was their friend who was so recently crucified. Hence his demand to see and touch the wounds of their master. A week later, he gets exactly what he wants. The one who appears to the community forced to meet behind locked doors can be no other than Jesus, who was crucified. That is what the sight of his wounds proves beyond doubt to Thomas. His scepticism has brought him to the place where he can believe the reports of Mary Magdalene and the other disciples, that they have indeed 'seen the Lord'. In the Johannine sense shown by the man born blind, Thomas can now 'see' with the insight that John calls faith. He sees and knows that 'I am in the Father and the Father is in me.' The words of his confession – 'My Lord and my God' – are a conduit to the beginning of the Gospel, with Sophia-Logos pitching her tent in the flesh and blood of Jesus. They also come as a sharp critique of the Emperor Domitian (AD 81-96), who demanded 'Lord and God' as his imperial title. Only the crucified and risen Jesus deserves this honour.[66]

---

66. Ironically, it was the emperor's representative Pontius Pilate who acknowledged the greater authority of Jesus when he insisted on crucifying him as 'King of the Jews'.

Reflections

In John's accounts of the way faith develops, he shows disciples dealing with a range of obstacles. The Samaritan woman works through the cultural and racial prejudices that separate her from the Jewish man Jesus. The man born blind stands up to his neighbours' cynicism and the authorities' hostile questioning. Mary of Bethany and Mary Magdalene struggle with their grief. Thomas lives with questions. His doubt is not so much a lack of trust in others or cynicism, but his desire for first- rather than second-hand faith. He has the courage to ask awkward questions of Jesus and to call his brother and sister disciples to account for what they believe. Only when he has made faith in Jesus his own ('*my* Lord and *my* God') does he reach the point of being able to trust what he has heard from the others.

Doubting like Thomas is a healthy ingredient of a living and developing faith, particularly when, as Bonhoeffer pointed out, the call of Jesus runs counter to secularised promises of happiness that bypass all talk of self-denial and self-giving. Thomas reminds us that God's costly grace means that faith must forever be asking questions, rather than seeking solace in answers.

Use the story of Thomas to reflect on the issues you find yourself working through on the way to a more confident faith. How much do the concerns raised in the stories of John's witnesses resonate with yours? What helps you to 'believe without seeing', on the basis of the story that goes back to Mary Magdalene and the other apostles, and what gets in the way? And what are the awkward questions that you and your faith community ask of the assumptions and values of your everyday world?

NINETEEN

Simon Peter

John 18:15-18, 25-27; 21:1-23

Background

Simon Peter is a prominent figure in the Gospels. In the synoptic Gospels he is a fisherman on the Sea of Galilee and one of the first to be called to follow Jesus. He is a member with James and John of the core group in the twelve disciples, and known for his sometimes unwelcome outspokenness. In Matthew 16:18, Jesus spotted his potential when the nickname he gave him identified his rough and unfinished faith as one of the foundations of the future of his movement. The story of Simon Peter and the other disciples is different in John's Gospel. Peter first meets Jesus in Judea, as one of John the Baptiser's followers. The twelve disciples do not have a core group. Peter makes no confession of faith in Jesus as messiah at Caesarea Philippi at the turning point of the narrative, though there are hints of this in his words after the feeding of the five thousand and the bread of life discourse: 'Lord, you have the words of eternal life. We have come to believe and know that you are the Holy One of God' (6:68, 69). Peter's three-fold denial remains (18:15-18, 25-27), supplemented by his exchange with Jesus over the washing of his feet at the Passover-tide supper (13:6-11), his identification as the disciple who cut off the ear of the high priest's slave when Jesus is arrested (18:10), and the poignancy of their conversation on the shore of the Sea of Tiberias (21:1-23).

John's account of the lakeside meeting does not easily fit with the accounts of resurrection appearances in the other Gospels, and Paul's statements in 1 Corinthians 15:5-8 only complicate matters further. The New Testament does not provide the raw materials for tidy chronologies of the startling new beginning we know as Easter. Chapter 21 looks like an afterthought; John 20:30, 31 reads like a natural ending, though there is no manuscript evidence that John's Gospel was ever published without it. The chapter certainly has a synoptic feel. It is similar to the story of Jesus meeting Peter in Luke 5:1-11, with its fruitless night on the lake followed by a remarkable catch, and the call of Peter to strike out in a new direction. The way it speaks of Jesus' coming in verse 22 is more like the synoptics' coming of the Son of Man than John's coming of Jesus in the Holy Spirit. It allows John to extend the resurrection appearances from Jerusalem to Galilee, where they are promised in Mark and narrated in Matthew.

If John 21 is based on material included in the synoptic Gospels, it might be a reflection on the hints of Peter's rehabilitation and future role in the words of the young man to the women at the tomb in Mark 16:7: 'go, tell his disciples and Peter that he is going ahead of you to Galilee; there you will see him, just as he told you'. If its author knows the story of Peter's call in Luke 5, he or she uses it to say that Jesus' last meeting with him is like the first. Peter's sense of unworthiness and his guilt do not have the last word. That lies with the gracious call of Jesus.

I imagine Peter recalling his time with Jesus, from their first meeting in the company of John the Baptiser, to their last by the Sea of Tiberias. Their relationship has always been challenging, never more so than Peter's call to go in yet another new direction.

Simon Peter's story

Fishing. I never really wanted to do anything else. My family has fished the Sea of Galilee for generations. We make a reasonable living. We're a big family. We have more fishermen than our boats will take. So we have an understanding. We pool what we earn and take what we need. We have time off from fishing now and then. We do other things. These last two years I seem to have been off the lake more than I've been out on it.

I first met Jesus near another stretch of water, in the south, on the edge of the desert, not far from where the Jordan flows into the Dead Sea. What's a fisherman doing out in the desert? Good question. I was coming back from one of the festivals in Jerusalem with my brother Andrew. While we were there we heard about a preacher called John, who was gathering crowds and baptising people across the Jordan. It was a bit of a detour, but we went to hear him. Even some of the priests were there. We stayed longer than we planned. There was something about the baptiser and his message that we couldn't get away from.

We were happy in Galilee. Happy in our work, more or less. But a lot of people I talk to say things can't go on forever, not the way they are under the Romans. I can't remember a time when they didn't rule us. They've done a lot for us – buildings, roads, peace – but at a price. They take more and more of what we earn in taxes. But not just our money. They've robbed us of our freedom. Sometimes I don't feel like we're living in our own land anymore. They act like they own it. They treat us like tenants.

Some Galileans say they'd like to force the Romans out, but let's be realistic, that's not going to happen. Their armies are too strong. When people get hot-headed, they crucify them, and leave their bodies hanging by the roadside – food for birds and wild animals – to show us who's in charge. It's shameful. 'Cursed is the body that hangs on a tree,' says Moses. Or as the Romans never cease to delight in reminding us, 'this is what happens when you step out of line'. It can't go on for ever.

John the baptiser was talking about things being different. He dressed and spoke like you imagine the old prophets did. He said he was preparing the way for God to come back to his people. He was calling everyone to get ready for this new future. God was about to send us a leader, he said. The Lamb of God, he called him. I'd heard that name before. Don't some say the messiah is the Lamb of God?

Andrew and I met the man that John was talking about. Jesus, from Nazareth, a Galilean like us. We started to follow him around Galilee with some others who'd been disciples of John, listening to him teach, watching him heal the sick. We travelled to the festivals in Jerusalem with him. We soon realised there was something of the rabbi and something of the prophet about him. It wasn't easy to pigeonhole him. He was interested in people, not violence. He had mixed feelings about the synagogue and the temple. He seemed to keep Moses' rules when it suited him, especially about the Sabbath. Sometimes he was easy to understand, sometimes a complete mystery. Like he was at the wedding up in Cana, when there was no wine and then more than we could drink. Or when he turned the tables on the moneychangers in Jerusalem, and said something about his body being the temple.

Once he fed a huge crowd on the other side of the lake with a few loaves and fishes. Word was going round that some of them wanted him to lead them against the Romans. He just disappeared. We had no idea where he was. We looked for him for ages. In the end it was so late we had to leave without him. We borrowed a boat to save us walking all the way round the lake. Everything was calm and clear when we set off, but then the wind blew up and we struggled with the boat. We were exhausted. We'd had a long day. We saw what looked like a figure walking on the sea, towards us. Was it real? Were we imagining it? Was it a ghost? Should we be scared? Before we could answer our questions, we were back at the shore. And there he was. A mystery.

I've never known a holy man mix so freely and openly with women, and not even respectable women at that. Samaritans, prostitutes. Mary Magdalene – some say she was possessed by devils when she first met Jesus, but look at her now. She's a new woman. She travels everywhere with us. Maybe his open-handed hospitality is why people feel so strongly about him. You either love him or loathe him. I've seen how most of our leaders in Jerusalem hate him. They were always arguing with him. They tried a few times to arrest him, and even stone him, but he always managed to escape. Until the Romans caught him in the garden.

The garden. That was quite a night. We'd come to Jerusalem for Passover. We'd not long finished our meal. His behaviour was unusual, even for him. He started acting like a slave, washing our feet. At first I said no, but then he insisted that if I didn't let him wash my feet I was as good as saying that I wanted nothing to do with him. That's the last thing I'd want. 'Wash me all over,' I said. Something was going on with Judas at the meal. We couldn't work it out. He left early, then Jesus turned on me and said that, before the night was out, I'd deny all knowledge of him. Why would he say that to me? I always spoke up for him. I even tried to fight off the people who came to arrest him, and even injured one of them with my sword. Jesus wasn't pleased. Not long after, I did what he told me I'd do. I said I didn't know him three times after he'd been arrested, when I was in the high priest's courtyard trying to keep warm by the fire. Three times I disowned him, just to save my skin.

I'll never forget what I said, standing by that charcoal fire. And how I ran away, back to the lodgings. 'Lie low till Passover's finished,' I told myself. 'Then back to Galilee, with Andrew and the others. There'll be enough pilgrims to give us cover.' But none of us reckoned with what happened next. The morning after the Sabbath . . . Mary Magdalene coming to tell us that his body had been stolen . . . running as fast as I could to the tomb, and finding it empty like she said . . . going back to the lodging . . . Mary coming back an hour or so later to say that she'd seen him . . . seeing him myself that evening, with all the others – except Thomas, he wasn't there . . . seeing him again a week later, with Thomas . . . then by the lake in Galilee after we'd finally got home safely.

Fishing again. A few of us had spent the night on the lake. What else were we supposed to do? We'd been waiting for ages for something to happen. Nothing. Fishing is what we do. It took my mind off things. It puts bread on the table. We were out all night on the lake. Nothing. Just as we were coming ashore – it must have been dawn – a man shouted to us: 'Cast your nets on the right side.' Perhaps he could see something we couldn't – a shoal of fish, maybe. But there was barely enough light. We did as he said. We'd nothing to lose. We caught enough to tear open the nets. But they were fine. Who was he? I remember someone on the boat shouting, 'It's the Lord!' Was it him, or a ghost, or just our imagination? There was only one way to find out. I put my tunic on. I jumped in, and waded to the shore.

And there he was, by a charcoal fire he'd lit, cooking fish. It brought back that night in Jerusalem, in the high priest's courtyard. I'll never forget what he said to me by the fire on the shore. Three times he asked if I loved him. Three times he told me to feed his flock. I had no idea what he meant at the time. I was a fisherman, not a shepherd. Three times he washed away my denials. Making me clean with his words. Cleaning not just my feet, but the whole of me. And then the mystery. There's no escaping the mystery with Jesus. Telling me someone would stretch out my hands when I got old. Calling me to follow him. Confusing me by saying something about the disciple he loved not dying. Then calling me again to follow him. And me wondering how a fisherman could turn into a shepherd.

How John uses the story of Simon Peter

Hints of Peter's future role in the story of the foot washing in 13:1-11 are amplified in the account of his visit to Jesus' tomb with the Beloved Disciple, following Mary Magdalene's startling discovery that the body had gone. Peter sees only an empty tomb, save for the grave clothes (20:6, 7). It is Mary who sees the risen Lord, and Thomas not Peter who makes the definitive confession of faith in Jesus, 'my Lord and my God' (20:28). Peter has no future until his triple disloyalty has been addressed.

John uses the story of the early morning lakeside breakfast to make two points. First, he reminds his audience of the earlier feeding of a much larger crowd on the other side of the lake, also with bread and fish (6:1-14). Both narratives stress the gift of food and its abundance. We are not told where the breakfast fish came from. Like the plenteous provision of bread and fish in the earlier story, and the best wine at the wedding in Cana, we can only assume that Jesus has supplied them. The number of 153 fish in verse 11 has long been a puzzle. Some say it refers to the number of known species of fish. If this is so, it symbolises the universal mission of Jesus, with the unbroken net signifying his desire to draw together one people, like the one flock in the parable of the Good Shepherd (10:16).

Secondly, the evangelist highlights the cleansing power of the word of Jesus (15:3), as the Lamb of God who takes away the sin of the world (1:29) deals with the particular sin of one of his closest followers. The links with Luke 5:1-11 draw out the meaning of Peter's rehabilitation. This is not simply forgiveness but re-commissioning, with a change in the imagery that symbolises his call: fishing in Luke 5, shepherding here. Peter is now free to play his part in the continuing mission of Jesus by extending the ministry of the Good Shepherd (21:15-19; see 10:1-18), though not without cost, for he too will lay down his life for the sheep. His re-call as a sign of Jesus' enduring faith in him would reassure those in the evangelist's audience who falter when their loyalty to Jesus is tested by the hostility of their local synagogue. Peter's story demonstrates that the last word lies not with human failure but with divine forgiveness, and that Jesus' care for his flock continues through the leaders of the community of Christ-followers (see 1 Peter 2:25; 5:1-4).

The ending of chapter 21 sweeps up a lingering concern in the evangelist's audience, the fate of the Beloved Disciple, whose testimony John has incorporated. Clearly Jesus' words about him – designed to keep Peter focused on his costly calling – have been misunderstood. The story of the raising of Lazarus suggests that the continuing experience of death was a cause for concern in early Christian communities. Yet even the Beloved Disciple must die. Jesus' last words in this Gospel can only cleanse the thoughts and feelings of those who have to reckon with the power, though not the ultimacy, of death.

Reflections

If we only read the other evangelists' accounts of Jesus' resurrection appearances, we might think that Easter faith is like something we order online. It arrives clearly addressed, neatly packaged and usually within a couple of days. John 21 suggests otherwise. The fact that Peter and the others return to Galilee and their fishing suggests that resurrection faith does not come quickly or easily. It moves this way and that, and takes time to grow and mature. Peter's story shows faith's vocational character. Peter is given the particular vocation to 'feed my sheep'. But Jesus' double call to 'follow me' in verses 19 and 22 returns to the beginning of John's story as it recalls Peter to the life of discipleship (1:43). A particular vocation to leadership in the Church is part of the wider vocation to discipleship. We could see the wider vocation to discipleship going further back to another beginning in the Bible, to the call that is issued to everyone who is made in the image of God (Genesis 1:26-31). Peter's vocation to 'feed my sheep' belongs with his vocation as a disciple, which is part of his more fundamental human vocation. This frees discipleship from a narrowly religious vision, and sees it as the servant of God's wider purposes, which for us include the care of the whole creation as well as of individuals.

It was Aristotle who saw vocation as the meeting place of human gifts and the needs of the world. A broader Christian understanding sees vocation as the way we respond to God's call whenever our gifts and passions engage with the opportunities and needs of the world. Peter's gifts and passions lay in fishing, yet Jesus saw his potential to be more than a fisherman. His story invites us to see our developing faith in Jesus as vocation in the broadest sense, the call to become truly human.

Use the story of Peter to reflect on your gifts and strengths, and the different worlds you occupy from day to day. How do your gifts and passions engage with these worlds? How much do you think you are being called to travel in the same direction as you look to the future, and how much to explore new paths?

TWENTY

The Beloved Disciple
John 13–17

Background

We have already noted that all four Gospels tell of Jesus' choosing twelve disciples from a wider group of followers. Twelve is a significant number for a people whose origins go back to the twelve sons of Jacob. By choosing twelve from among so many, Jesus signals his intention to renew Israel as God's people. In the synoptic Gospels and Acts 1, the twelve are named.[67] They appear in much the same order, and eleven disciples are included in all four lists. Thaddeus is mentioned in Matthew and Mark, but not in the lists in Luke and Acts, whose 'Judas the son of James' may be the same person.

Other disciples are also named in the synoptic Gospels. In Mark 2:14, Jesus calls Levi the tax collector to follow him (Matthew names him 'Matthew' and includes him in his list of the twelve). Luke 8:1-4 records the names of three of the women who followed Jesus around Galilee and funded his itinerant band: Mary Magdalene, Joanna the wife of Herod's steward Chuza, and Susanna. This Mary appears with another Mary and Salome, together with other unnamed Galilean women, in the accounts of Jesus' crucifixion, watching from a distance, and the named women go to Jesus' tomb once the Sabbath is over to anoint his body. Luke 10:38-42 also suggests that the sisters Martha and Mary are disciples, as are Cleopas and his companion, whom Jesus meets on the road to Emmaus in Luke 24:13-35.

The Gospel of John refers to the twelve four times in 6:67-71 and 20:24, though he has no account of their being specially chosen and no list of their names. He mentions Simon Peter, Andrew, Philip, Nathanael (who is not in the other evangelists' lists), Thomas, the sons of Zebedee (not named, but presumably James and John), Judas Iscariot, two other unnamed disciples who are in Peter's fishing party in John 21, and the mysterious 'disciple whom Jesus loved' (the Beloved Disciple) who only appears in John. There are other disciples who are outside this inner core: Nicodemus and Joseph of Arimathea, the Bethany family (Mary, Martha and Lazarus), and the unnamed disciple known to the high priest who obtains access for Peter to the high priest's courtyard after Jesus' arrest (18:15).

The identity of the Beloved Disciple has been a source of speculation from at least the second century. Was he the evangelist or the apostle

---

67. Matthew 10:1-4; Mark 3:13-19; Luke 6:12-16; Acts 1:13.

John (if these were not the same person), or even Mark or Paul or Apollos? Some think that Lazarus was the Beloved Disciple because he is referred to as 'he whom you love' in his sisters' message to Jesus (11:3). But with such a strong clue, why does John then keep his identity secret when he mentions him later? The Beloved Disciple appears at the Passover-tide supper, where he is particularly close to Jesus.[68] He is at the cross with the mother of Jesus and a group of other women, and may be the one who witnesses Jesus' death.[69] On the day after the Sabbath, he races to Jesus' tomb with Peter to check Mary Magdalene's story that it has been disturbed and the body stolen.[70] He is the disciple in Peter's fishing party who recognises the figure by the Sea of Tiberias as 'the Lord'.[71] He appears at the end of that story as the disciple following Jesus and Peter as they walk along the shore. The evangelist ends his Gospel by identifying him as a true witness who has written down what he has seen and heard (21:20-24).

In what follows, I assume that the Beloved Disciple is one of the evangelist's principal sources and strongest influences, particularly in his account of Jesus' words at his final Passover-tide meal in chapters 13–17. I imagine him meditating on some of Jesus' words and actions from the end of his ministry – his promise of the Holy Spirit in times of adversity, his talk of the coming of the Son of Man, his call to live like slaves, his prayer for Peter and the others – so that Jesus continues to abide in a new audience.[72] In all this he is a creative yet trustworthy interpreter of Jesus, reflecting here on his contribution to the work of re-telling the story of Jesus for new audiences, and sharing his thoughts with the writer of the Gospel.

The Beloved Disciple's story

I've never been one for jumping to conclusions. I prefer to hold things in my mind and heart for a while. People say I have a good memory. But I don't just remember. I see and hear new things. I make new connections. That happens all the time with what I saw and heard in Jesus.

The way he taught was a gift for someone like me. All those sayings and stories. Sometimes they were entertaining, sometimes teasing, sometimes shocking and provocative. There was always more than we saw on the surface. That was his genius. It's why he always had the last word. We never felt we'd heard the end of his sayings. Let them get under your skin, he told us. Listen, then listen again for the mystery they reveal.

---

68. In John 13:23, he is said to be 'in the bosom of Jesus', just as Jesus is 'in the bosom of the Father' in 1:18.
69. John 19:25-27, 35. In the synoptic Gospels, the male disciples have fled and the Galilean women disciples are watching from a distance.
70. John 20:1-10; the account of this visit to the tomb by male disciples only appears in John.
71. John 21:7; his words echo those of Mary Magdalene and the male disciples in Jerusalem in 20:18, 25, 28.
72. See Mark 13:9-13, 24-27; Luke 22:24-27, 31, 32.

He often told stories about landowners or kings who went away for a while. They trusted their servants to look after their interests, and then they came back to find out what they'd been up to. It's a great story line. It helped me to picture Jesus' coming and going. When things were getting hot between him and the Pharisees, he'd talk about going away. 'I am going away and you will search for me, but you will die in your sin. Where I am going you cannot come.' They had no idea what he meant. It was one of those sayings that went round and round in my head. Then one day it clicked.

Coming and going. That summed him up. He came from heaven, like Sophia in Solomon's poems. Feeding us with the bread and wine of God's wisdom. Teaching us the true ways of God. It took a while to work out what he meant when he talked about coming and going. But Sophia helped me to see and hear and understand.

He went away from us when he died, like everyone does when they die. But of course he didn't just die, and he didn't just go. His life was taken from him. We could see it coming. One day his enemies would get what they wanted, get what they needed to keep the peace in Jerusalem. But was it really taken from him, or did he give it?

I remember the stories he told about looking after sheep. How the shepherd searched everywhere for the one that got lost. Ridiculous really. No shepherd I know would leave his flock to look for just one sheep. But that was the point. His story shook me into seeing him as the true shepherd, the good shepherd, who led his flock out of the sheepfold in search of pasture and brought them back safely every night. He even laid down his life like shepherds did every night when they slept across the gate of the sheepfold to protect the flock, and then got up again to start a new day. The rhythms of coming and going, descending and ascending summed up the way he gave himself perfectly.

Then there were the stories he told about farming. He understood how risky it is to grow things. The seeds don't always produce the harvest we need. The soil may not be good enough, the weeds get in the way, the weather lets us down. I began to see him in the seed that fell into the ground, like Sophia descending from heaven, to grow into wheat for the bread of eternal life. I imagined him as the vine in the story he told to the authorities about the vineyard. God's true vine, growing grapes for Sophia's rich wine, his own poured-out blood. Holding his followers and friends together as if we were grape-bearing branches.

When he was talking to us at the end, I started thinking about our ancestors Jacob and Moses. Jacob gathered all his sons together and blessed them. Moses reminded the people of God's commandments – all his blessings and judgements – before they came into the land God gave them. Isn't that what Jesus did before he went? He gathered us all together and promised to bless us, even though he was about to be taken from us. He gave us a new commandment to love each other like he loved us. And that way we'd extend his blessing into the world.

I remembered some of the other things he said before he went away. I let them get to work on me. 'It won't be easy for you,' he said. 'The authorities will come after you too. But don't worry what to say. The Holy Spirit will give you the words you need.' Then when we started arguing with each other about who would have pride of place in God's kingdom, he talked about the greatness of slaves. I'd never heard a rabbi speak like that before. When Peter was full of himself at the last meal, Jesus saw right through his bravado and promised to pray for him, that his faith would stay strong.

I thought again about Jesus' going away and coming back to bless us. No promised land for us, just the Holy Spirit, who gives us the words we need. I heard Jesus speaking about going to his Father's house and coming back to take us with him. Not taking us out of the world we know, but coming to us in the Holy Spirit – that's how he would take us to the Father's house. The Holy Spirit is his coming. The Holy Spirit is Jesus abiding in us, just like the Holy Spirit was God abiding in him. The Holy Spirit is the new presence of Jesus in us. Speaking to us like an advocate in a court room. Helping us to remember and understand the truth in what he was saying when he was with us before he died. Giving us the courage to speak up for him to those who condemned and even attacked us. Even making it possible for us to know God like he did, as our Father who loves us more than we'll ever realise.

Love. Moses said a lot about loving God and loving others, even loving strangers and foreigners. I see Jesus showing us what true love for God looks like. And how that makes all the difference to the way we are with one another. The bread and wine from the Passover meal, like the bread feeding the crowd up in Galilee. Sophia's feast, nourishing us in God's wise ways. Jesus giving his flesh-and-blood life. Giving himself by acting like a slave washing his disciples' feet. Rabbis don't do the work of slaves. But our rabbi Jesus did, and shocked us into seeing him give his whole life away. 'Love one another, as I have loved you. There is no greater love than giving your life away for your friends.'

Jesus is still speaking. Still feeding us with his poured-out life. Still praying for all of us. 'I have prayed for you, Peter, that your faith may not fail.' I was always impressed by the way he prayed. Not just in the synagogue and the temple with other people, but on his own, in the desert, before the day started, with the people he touched and healed, with us whenever he said grace over a meal. When we asked him to teach us how to pray, he taught us some words we could use. Full of pictures as usual, but deep just the same. Watching him pray made me realise that prayer is much more than words. It's about learning to live what we pray, and pray what we live. I see his going away as a great prayer. The life he gave is his prayer for us to be faithful to God like he was. To love each other in the way that he did. Even to share something of the glory he now enjoys in the bosom of his heavenly Father.

My friend John is writing an account of Jesus. He came to talk to me about it. He asked me what I could remember. When I told him I had a good memory and that I see and hear new things, he said that's just what he wanted. He's hoping to write something people can trust. A Gospel that will bring the story of Jesus to life for people who don't know him like we do. A true witness that will help them to believe in the living presence of Jesus as God's anointed Son. He made some notes, and I lent him my manuscripts. We agreed to meet again once we'd both had time to remember what we'd seen and heard.

How John uses the Beloved Disciple's story

The Beloved Disciple only appears in the second half of the Gospel, during the final hours of Jesus' earthly life and in one of the risen Jesus' appearances to his disciples. His association with the twin themes of revelation and discipleship qualifies him as a trustworthy witness to Jesus, and a reliable source of John's Gospel. John introduces him in 13:23 at the final Passover-tide meal. Jesus and the disciples are reclining, in typical Greco-Roman fashion, and the Beloved Disciple has his head by Jesus' chest. Jesus has just announced that one of the disciples will betray him to the authorities, and Peter wants to know who it is. Instead of asking Jesus directly, he relies on the Beloved Disciple to find out. Though Jesus' response is ambiguous, it is enough to reveal the identity of his betrayer. The Beloved Disciple, reclining 'in the bosom of Jesus', reveals the mind of his Lord, just as 'the Son who is close to the Father's bosom' (the English translation of 1:18 has 'heart') reveals the truth of God.

The Beloved Disciple's sensitivity to divine revelation comes across again in two of John's Easter stories. When Mary Magdalene finds that Jesus' tomb has been disturbed, she reports the matter to Simon Peter and the Beloved Disciple (20:1-10). The two men run to the tomb, and the Beloved Disciple arrives first. He looks into the tomb, but waits for Peter to arrive before entering. Both men see Jesus' discarded grave clothes, but only the Beloved Disciple 'saw and believed' (20:8). But what did he believe? Some commentators think that the Beloved Disciple is the first to believe that Jesus has been raised from the dead. But others fasten onto the suggestion in verse 9 that neither of the men believed this, 'for as yet they did not understand the scripture, that he must rise from the dead'. Both men return home with a distinct lack of the strong emotions that accompany the beginnings of resurrection faith elsewhere in the New Testament. The Beloved Disciple certainly believes Mary's story, while Peter does not seem to know what to make of it. Perhaps the most we can say of the Disciple is that he appears to be more open to resurrection faith than Peter, but in this Gospel it is Mary Magdalene who is its first witness.

There is no doubting the Beloved Disciple's resurrection faith in the later story of Jesus' appearance by the Sea of Tiberias, after a group of disciples have a fruitless night's fishing.[73] The Disciple is one of a group of seven disciples who go fishing at Simon Peter's instigation. As they are preparing to land their empty boat at sunrise, a man they do not recognise calls to them from the shore and tells them to fish from the right side. Now they catch too many fish to land. It is the Beloved Disciple who recognises the figure immediately, and tells Peter, 'It is the Lord.' The description of the Beloved Disciple as the one who reveals something of Jesus to Peter recalls the scene at the Passover-tide supper.

The Beloved Disciple's final appearance comes at the end of chapter 21, after Peter's conversation with Jesus by the lake (21:20-24). Peter is not surprisingly shaken by Jesus' announcement of the costly consequences of the loyalty he has just professed, and finds a ready diversion in the presence of the Beloved Disciple who is walking behind them. Jesus' reply gave rise to a rumour that this disciple would still be alive at his coming on the day of judgement. John takes the opportunity to correct this misunderstanding, and at the same time underline the importance of the Beloved Disciple as the source of true testimony to Jesus. Verse 24 has been used by some as evidence that the Beloved Disciple is the author of the Gospel. But the distinction between 'the disciple who is testifying to these things and has written them' and 'we [who] know that his testimony is true' suggests that the evangelist has been drawing on trustworthy sources provided by the Beloved Disciple, whose authority flows from the intimacy of his relationship with Jesus.

John's insistence on connecting the Beloved Disciple, true testimony and the writing of the Gospel is highly significant in view of the way his Gospel tells the story of Jesus. So much that is familiar from the other Gospels is not found in John, including such foundational material as the Lord's Prayer, the parables, Jesus' teaching about the coming kingdom of God and the institution of the Eucharist. John re-interprets Jesus' teaching about his coming on the day of judgement, and sees this largely realised in the coming of the Holy Spirit. What John does include heightens the authority of Jesus, and at the same time runs the risk of restricting discipleship to those who hold what the evangelist considers to be the right beliefs about Jesus. As we have noted throughout this book, there are good reasons for John's re-shaping of the story of Jesus. If John wrote his Gospel at a time when most of the earliest eye-witnesses were dead, the testimony of the Beloved Disciple could only lend weight to the authority of such a radical revision, by rooting it in the witness of one who was very close to its central character when it mattered most.

---

73. John 21:1-14; the story is similar to the account of Peter's call in Luke 5:1-11, and is the only one of Jesus' three resurrection appearances in this Gospel to take place in Galilee.

Finally, John's stress on the authority of the Beloved Disciple is important because he is the centrepiece of an egalitarian vision of discipleship that struggled to establish itself in the early Jesus movement. Only in this Gospel does the dying Jesus bequeath his mother and the male disciple he loves to each other, in his 'Woman, behold your son . . . Behold your mother' (19:25-27). The evangelist sees a new family of disciples coming into being around the cross. These women and men are joined not by traditional ties but by the call of Jesus. Like the faithful disciples of Sophia in Proverbs 4:6, they refuse to forsake him. The presence of women here, two of whom are named, serves to raise the profile of women as disciples, something that is established throughout the Gospel by the prominence of the mother of Jesus, the Samaritan woman, Mary and Martha, and Mary Magdalene. By contrast, women are entirely absent from the appendix to the Gospel. Here the focus of discipleship shifts to more traditional territory, with its concerns about male leadership. So the presence of the Beloved Disciple at the beginning and the end of chapter 21 is a way of ensuring that John's more radical vision of discipleship is not lost.

The mystery of the identity of the Beloved Disciple remains. Is this anonymous disciple a real, flesh-and-blood figure or an ideal image of the discipleship that lives close to Jesus, ever-receptive to what he may wish to reveal? A stronger case for the Beloved Disciple as an ideal or representative follower of Jesus could be made if this disciple appeared more regularly in the Gospel, alongside the others whom Jesus chose. By including him where he does, John seems to see him not so much as an ideal disciple as a true and trustworthy witness to the ongoing life of Jesus, rooted as it is in his passion. What comes from the Beloved Disciple comes ultimately from Jesus, which both encourages and limits the creativity that is necessary if the story of Jesus is to speak to new audiences.

Reflections

What makes a painting, a piece of music, a film, a novel or a poem a classic? Some would say its quality, others might argue for its appeal. Classics of whatever kind are those that we go back to again and again. We find a freshness in them each time. They speak to us in new ways as circumstances change. What they mean has not been determined by whoever has produced them. There seems to be a surplus of meaning that overflows into new situations.

If scriptures are collections of classic texts for communities of faith, we should expect them also to have a surplus of meaning. My interpretation of the work of the Beloved Disciple assumes that he delivers to the author of John's Gospel some of the surplus that is emerging in his day from his reflection on the classic words and works of Jesus, particularly at the end of his ministry. The Beloved

Disciple is an instrument of the Holy Spirit, taking what he hears and sees of Jesus and drawing out its meaning for new audiences of disciples (16:13-15).

On this understanding, the Gospel of John is not an end in itself. It suggests ways in which we might read the other Gospels, and indeed the rest of the Bible, in circumstances that are quite different from those in which its writings were first put together. Stay for the moment, though, with John's Gospel. As you have been reading it through its long line of witnesses, which particular aspects of the surplus of meaning he finds in Jesus have caught your attention? How will you allow this surplus to overflow into the way you practise your faith with others, and in your everyday life in the world?

Conclusion
The Abiding Spirit of Jesus

Developing faith in Jesus

The purpose of John's Gospel is to commend faith in Jesus Christ, the Son of God. At the start of this book, I said that this either means confirming people in what they already believe or converting them to something that they have yet to embrace. My reading of John leans more towards confirmation than conversion, though I can imagine the stories of his characters contributing to either or even both of these possibilities. As we have explored their witness, we have seen the way John presents faith as a living, developing reality. In narrative time, most of John's witnesses soon reach their conclusions about Jesus. But this, I said, was the consequence of his desire to show that the DNA of their faith is present from the beginning.

The Gospel of John is not a study of the sequence of faith development in the manner of James Fowler and John Westerhoff.[74] John's sketches of people such as the Samaritan woman, the man born blind, Mary and Martha, Mary Magdalene and Thomas, outline some of the key components of living faith. His witnesses begin to respond to Jesus when they meet him as a human person where they are. John situates Jesus in locations defined as much by social and economic status, inherited attitudes, strong emotions and political structures as by geography, and these meeting places become ground in which faith can grow. As they engage in the give-and-take of conversation and questioning, John's characters start to see Jesus as more than a Jewish man or a Galilean rabbi, more even than their best friend. They often have to struggle against obstacles of their own or other people's making, or the impact of everyday experiences such as loss and prejudice. They eventually express their faith in Jesus in language that would have been known in the circles for whom John writes. Their Jesus is the promised prophet or messiah, the son of God, the king of Israel, the saviour of the world. Mary Magdalene goes one stage further by being the first to recognise her crucified rabbi now raised from the dead as 'the Lord', and Thomas' climactic acknowledgement of him as 'my Lord and my God' gathers up everything that others have said and presents it as the summit and summation of Johannine faith.

Whatever these terms may have meant to others both within and beyond the Jesus movement, they receive their Johannine significance

---

74. James Fowler, Stages of Faith: *The Psychology of Human Development and the Quest for Meaning*, HarperCollins, 1995 (new English edition); John Westerhoff, *Will Our Children Have Faith?* Morehouse Publishing, 2012 (3rd revised edition).

from the theological framework that the evangelist uses to structure his work. Jesus is the one in whose flesh and blood the heavenly Sophia-Logos of God descends to pitch her tent, before ascending back to the bosom of the Father once his work is finished. He is the Lamb of God who takes away the sins of the world in the hour of his glorious crucifixion. He does the work of God because he is equal to the Father and one with God. And in his 'I am' statements and sayings, he reveals the divine presence and speaks with an authority that calls into question all human powers and rulers. Creative rather than inventive, John develops material found elsewhere that speaks of Jesus as the one in whom God's promise is fulfilled and his kingdom realised. The evangelist's testimony stretches language into new shapes to express his faith that Jesus mediates the highest authority imaginable.

John's developing faith in Jesus is not for isolated individuals. Neither is what they come to believe a private affair. His characters are all members of public communities of faith into which they are born from above, whether as villagers in Samaria, much-loved disciples in Bethany, friends who share Passover-tide table fellowship with Jesus or members of the new family that comes into being around the cross. The various components of their faith are not so much stages on the road to spiritual maturity as dimensions of a dynamic and resilient witness to Jesus Christ, the Son of God.

Ethical Christology, trinitarian spirituality

I said at the start of this book that John's Gospel is both theological and spiritual. These characteristics focus on Christology. Johannine faith finds ever richer expression in its understanding of who Jesus is and where he is from. But this is an ethical Christology. Jesus is not simply the name above all names, but the one who is granted the ultimate authority to shape and direct human life. John's developing faith in Jesus expresses itself not simply in confessions of who Jesus is but in the practice of Christ-like living.

Unlike the synoptic Gospels, the spirituality of John does not fuse the call to love God and neighbour or extend love to enemies. But Jesus' new commandment to 'love one another as I have loved you' is anything but sectarian. We saw in the discussion of the bread of life discourse that eucharistic living shows itself as loving solidarity with those branches on the true vine who, like the man born blind, are excluded from the synagogue on account of their openly professed loyalty to Jesus. The Gospel as a whole suggests that this same spirit of loving solidarity should also find expression in the readiness to cross social and cultural boundaries around gender, race and disability, as it did in Jesus.

Yet John's ethical Christology is more than mere imitation of Christ. Its inspiration comes from the Holy Spirit, bestowed on the disciples by the risen Christ as the breath of his resurrection and life.

John's understanding of the Holy Spirit develops ideas that are found elsewhere in the New Testament: Paul's Spirit of Christ whose harvest is the Christ-like qualities of faith, hope and love (Romans 8:9-12; Galatians 5:22-25); Luke's gift of the ascended Jesus, who reproduces his Galilean ministry in Jerusalem in the aftermath of Pentecost (Acts 2–4). As he does in his Christology, John explores his understanding of the Holy Spirit by drawing on the poetry of Sophia, who 'passes into holy souls and makes them friends of God' (Wisdom 7:27). The farewell speeches in chapters 14–16 hold out a promise of the Spirit that is more about abiding presence than unrestrained energy. John the Baptiser has seen the Spirit come to rest (the Greek verb is menein, also translated as 'abide') on Jesus at his baptism. As he approaches the hour when his work is accomplished, Jesus promises that the same Spirit of God who abides in him will come to abide in his friends forever, and introduce them into the relationship he enjoys with his heavenly Father. The community that loves him and keeps his word will even go on to extend his works and teaching, because the Spirit will be another advocate, one like him who comes from the Father and acts on his behalf.

The coming of the Holy Spirit imbues the faith of Jesus' followers with what we might now call a trinitarian character. Just as the Spirit abides in Jesus and enables him to call God 'Father', so the same Spirit comes to those who live by his commandment, as the abiding presence of the Father and the Son in the eternal communion of love. It is as if Jesus' experience of his Father's love in the baptismal Spirit is reproduced in his followers. In stark contrast with so much that passes for spirituality in postmodern settings, Johannine spirituality is fundamentally God-shaped.

A new presence of Jesus

John sees the Holy Spirit bringing about a new and abiding presence of the crucified and exalted Jesus in the community of his friends, and at the same time opening a new chapter in the story of Sophia-Logos at work in God's creation. This is why the disciples are not abandoned, despite his going away. The one who lived alongside them, and whose memory they cherish, now lives in and through them as the love of God for the world. But there is a downside. This new presence of Jesus draws the same hostile response from his enemies that Jesus of Nazareth drew to himself. So it is important that they do not allow the world's judgement to be decisive. It did not have the last word on Jesus, as his resurrection shows, and it must not have the last word on them. They are to see the coming of God's Spirit not only as an abiding appearance of the exalted Jesus in the world, but also as an extended vindication of all that he lived and died for. Like the parousia[75] of the

---

75. The Greek word *parousia* means 'presence' or 'arrival'. In Christian theology, it is mainly used to refer to the 'second coming' of Jesus at the end of time. Some theologians are unwilling to restrict Christ's coming to a single event, and include Easter and Pentecost in his *parousia*.

Son of Man on the day of judgement in the other Gospels, the coming of the Holy Spirit is the source of hope as well as comfort for the friends and followers of Jesus.

The promise of the Holy Spirit sheds fresh light on one of this Gospel's most intriguing themes, the hope-filled absence of Jesus. We saw how on three occasions John explores the significance of the absence of Jesus when people are threatened by death. The royal official's son in Capernaum is at the point of death, and Jesus refuses to come from Cana where he is staying. Later on, his beloved friend Lazarus is seriously ill in Bethany, and initially Jesus again refuses to travel to a dying person, this time from his place of safety across the Jordan. At their tense final Passover-tide meal, Jesus' disciples rehearse not only their own fears but also those from John's audience, where distress is fuelled by the hostility of the local synagogue and aggravated by the physical absence of Jesus. The first two occasions show Jesus having the last word over death, despite his distance and delayed response. On the third occasion, as Jesus prepares to leave his disciples, he promises that the Holy Spirit 'will take what is mine and declare it to you' (16:14). As the new and abiding presence of Jesus, the Spirit brings the words of Jesus to life in new situations, by extending their death-defying power from Cana and Capernaum and Bethany to wherever his disciples are. So by paving the way for the coming of the Spirit, Jesus' return to his heavenly Father can only mean that trinitarian spirituality is forever hope-filled.

It is stretching John's understanding of the abiding Spirit of Jesus to view his coming as a new divine incarnation, but the evangelist comes as close as he dares to seeing it in these terms. He is restrained by his insistence on maintaining the distance between Jesus and his disciples, which is at least as great in his Gospel as it is in Mark's. For all their expressions of faith and loyalty, they depend entirely on Jesus. 'Apart from me you can do nothing, [because] you did not choose me, I chose you' (15:5, 16). With its unwavering focus on Jesus, John's theological and spiritual Gospel has one of the richest understandings of God and human wellbeing in the whole of the New Testament. His vision of the abiding Spirit of Jesus at the heart of an ethical Christology and a trinitarian spirituality fulfils Sophia's offer of the finest wine and bread enough for all, and her promise of life in all its fullness.

Epilogue

In the beginning was the Spirit.
The Spirit is from God
and the Spirit is God,
because God is Spirit.
All things come to life through the Spirit
and without God's breath there is nothing.

There was a man sent from God whose name was John. He came as a witness to testify to the Spirit, so that all might be born of water and Spirit. The Spirit was not from John, but he came to testify to the abiding Spirit.

The Spirit has always been at work in the world,
full of mystery, like the wind.
Making holy souls into friends of God and prophets,
flowing like water from the wounded Son,
breath of peace and new beginnings.
No one has ever seen God.
It is God who is Spirit
who leads the way to the Father's house,
the temple where all who are born from above
offer the fragrant sacrifice of love
that flows between Father and Son
and abides forever in the Spirit.

Appendix

The Poetry of Wisdom

The Gospel of John makes extensive use of Jewish Wisdom writings in the way it tells the story of Jesus. Rather than overload the text of this book with extensive quotations, the main background material is printed here. Reading longer sections rather than fragments of Wisdom poetry gives a flavour of its general outlook, particularly in its later writings.

The Jewish Wisdom writings are eclectic collections of material drawn from the wider near eastern world. They include pithy sayings based on observation and reflection, poems and prayers for wisdom. Their theological texture varies, with some of the sayings in particular making little or no mention of God. But the body of work as a whole assumes that God is the source of wisdom, and that a spiritual disposition is necessary in order to be wise. This is well expressed in Proverbs 1:7: 'The fear of the Lord is the beginning of knowledge; fools despise wisdom and instruction.'

Wisdom is a divine attribute. God is wise in the way he orders the world, and those who discover and live by his wisdom will find the life for which they are made, as this poem shows:

> The LORD by wisdom founded the earth;
>   by understanding he established the heavens;
> by his knowledge the deeps broke open,
>   and the clouds drop down the dew.
>
> My child, do not let these escape from your sight:
>   keep sound wisdom and prudence,
> and they will be life for your soul
>   and adornment for your neck.
>
> *Proverbs 3:19-22*

Solomon reigned from about 970-930 BC, and is the fount of wisdom in the same way that Moses is the great lawgiver (1 Kings 4:29-34). Like the laws attributed to Moses, some Wisdom writings associated with Solomon are much later than his day. Ecclesiastes is from the 3rd century BC and the Wisdom of Solomon from the 1st century BC. Throughout the Wisdom writings, wisdom is seen in personal rather than abstract terms, often as a woman who makes her appeal and offers her teachings in the public world. God's desire is to share his wisdom with humankind, but wisdom's offer brings division. Those who welcome wisdom live in security and peace. Those who refuse her call down God's judgement upon themselves. John the evangelist sees Jesus' ministry having the same outcome.

This poem celebrates the fruits of embracing and rejecting wisdom. Righteous living and just rule are sharply contrasted with pride, arrogance and evil speech. The relationship between wisdom and those who welcome her is one of mutual love, as is Jesus' relationship with his disciples in John 13–17:

Does not Sophia[76] call,
    and does not understanding raise her voice?
On the heights, beside the way,
    at the crossroads she takes her stand;
beside the gates in front of the town,
    at the entrance of the portals she cries out:
'To you, O people, I call,
    and my cry is to all that live.
O simple ones, learn prudence;
    acquire intelligence, you who lack it.
Hear, for I will speak noble things,
    and from my lips will come what is right;
for my mouth will utter truth;
    wickedness is an abomination to my lips.
All the words of my mouth are righteous;
    there is nothing twisted or crooked in them.
They are all straight to one who understands
    and right to those who find knowledge.
Take my instruction instead of silver,
    and knowledge rather than choice gold;
for wisdom is better than jewels,
    and all that you may desire cannot compare with her.
I, Sophia, live with prudence,
    and I attain knowledge and discretion.
The fear of the LORD is hatred of evil.
Pride and arrogance and the way of evil
    and perverted speech I hate.
I have good advice and sound wisdom;
    I have insight, I have strength.
By me kings reign,
    and rulers decree what is just;
by me rulers rule,
    and nobles, all who govern rightly.
I love those who love me,
    and those who seek me diligently find me.
Riches and honour are with me,
    enduring wealth and prosperity.

---

76. I have replaced 'wisdom' with 'Sophia' where the poems personify God's wisdom.

My fruit is better than gold, even fine gold,
   and my yield than choice silver.
I walk in the way of righteousness,
   along the paths of justice,
endowing with wealth those who love me,
   and filling their treasuries.

      Proverbs 8:1-21

The mutual love of Sophia and her disciples (her 'children', as Jesus calls his disciples in John 13:33) is also a theme in this later poem from Ecclesiasticus (2nd century BC):

Sophia teaches her children
   and gives help to those who seek her.
Whoever loves her loves life,
   and those who seek her from early morning are filled with joy.
Whoever holds her fast inherits glory,
   and the Lord blesses the place she enters.
Those who serve her minister to the Holy One;
   the Lord loves those who love her.
Those who obey her will judge the nations,
   and all who listen to her will live secure.

      Ecclesiasticus 4:11-15

Wisdom's offer of life is symbolised here by the feast. Her invitation to partake of her bread and wine to those who walk in her ways lies behind Jesus' offering his bread and wine to his disciples in John 6:25-59:

Wisdom has built her house,
   she has hewn her seven pillars.
She has slaughtered her animals, she has mixed her wine,
   she has also set her table.
She has sent out her servant-girls, she calls
   from the highest places in the town,
'You that are simple, turn in here!'
   To those without sense she says,
'Come, eat of my bread
   and drink of the wine I have mixed.
Lay aside immaturity, and live,
   and walk in the way of insight.'

      Proverbs 9:1-6

This poem brings out the stark contrast between the ways of wisdom and folly. The metaphorical use of light and darkness at the end of this section lies behind Jesus' words in John 11:9, 10 and 12:35-50:

Do not forsake Sophia, and she will keep you;
 love her, and she will guard you.
Prize her highly, and she will exalt you;
 she will honour you if you embrace her.
She will place on your head a fair garland;
 she will bestow on you a beautiful crown.

Hear, my child, and accept my words,
 that the years of your life may be many.
I have taught you the way of Sophia;
 I have led you in the paths of uprightness.
When you walk, your step will not be hampered;
 and if you run, you will not stumble.
Keep hold of instruction; do not let go;
 guard her, for she is your life.
Do not enter the path of the wicked,
 and do not walk in the way of evildoers.
Avoid it; do not go on it;
 turn away from it and pass on.
For they cannot sleep unless they have done wrong;
 they are robbed of sleep unless they have made someone stumble.
For they eat the bread of wickedness
 and drink the wine of violence.
But the path of the righteous is like the light of dawn,
 which shines brighter and brighter until full day.
The way of the wicked is like deep darkness;
 they do not know what they stumble over.

Proverbs 4:6, 8-19

Wisdom's work in creation is elevated in this poem. Here she speaks as a heavenly being, the first of God's creative works:

The Lord created me at the beginning of his work,
 the first of his acts of long ago.
Ages ago I was set up,
 at the first, before the beginning of the earth.
When there were no depths I was brought forth,
 when there were no springs abounding with water.
Before the mountains had been shaped,
 before the hills, I was brought forth –
when he had not yet made earth and fields,
 or the world's first bits of soil.
When he established the heavens, I was there,
 when he drew a circle on the face of the deep,
when he made firm the skies above,
 when he established the fountains of the deep,

when he assigned to the sea its limit,
    so that the waters might not transgress his command,
when he marked out the foundations of the earth,
    then I was beside him, like a master worker;
and I was daily his delight,
    rejoicing before him always,
rejoicing in his inhabited world
    and delighting in the human race.

Proverbs 8:22-31

Later Wisdom writings develop the image of heavenly wisdom. Not only is she God's agent in creation, she is also at work in the story of Israel. This poem is from Ecclesiasticus, written in Greek in the second century BC for Jews living in Egypt. Here universal wisdom is particularly focused on Israel, and available to those who live by the law of Moses. John the evangelist borrows the language of Sophia's descent and tent-dwelling when he writes of the heavenly Word's taking flesh and 'living' among us (John 1:14). There are also echoes here of Jesus' talk of eating and drinking, and of himself as living water and the true vine:

Sophia praises herself,
    and tells of her glory in the midst of her people.
In the assembly of the Most High she opens her mouth,
    and in the presence of his hosts she tells of her glory:
'I came forth from the mouth of the Most High,
    and covered the earth like a mist.
I dwelt in the highest heavens,
    and my throne was in a pillar of cloud.
Alone I compassed the vault of heaven
    and traversed the depths of the abyss.
Over waves of the sea, over all the earth,
    and over every people and nation I have held sway.
Among all these I sought a resting-place;
    in whose territory should I abide?

'Then the Creator of all things gave me a command,
    and my Creator chose the place for my tent.
He said, "Make your dwelling in Jacob,
    and in Israel receive your inheritance."
Before the ages, in the beginning, he created me,
    and for all the ages I shall not cease to be.
In the holy tent I ministered before him,
    and so I was established in Zion.
Thus in the beloved city he gave me a resting-place,
    and in Jerusalem was my domain.
I took root in an honoured people,
    in the portion of the Lord, his heritage.

'I grew tall like a cedar in Lebanon,
    and like a cypress on the heights of Hermon.
I grew tall like a palm tree in En-gedi,
    and like rose-bushes in Jericho;
like a fair olive tree in the field,
    and like a plane tree beside water I grew tall.
Like cassia and camel's thorn I gave forth perfume,
    and like choice myrrh I spread my fragrance,
like galbanum, onycha, and stacte,
    and like the odour of incense in the tent.
Like a terebinth I spread out my branches,
    and my branches are glorious and graceful.
Like the vine I bud forth delights,
    and my blossoms become glorious and abundant fruit.

'Come to me, you who desire me,
    and eat your fill of my fruits.
For the memory of me is sweeter than honey,
    and the possession of me sweeter than the honeycomb.
Those who eat of me will hunger for more,
    and those who drink of me will thirst for more.
Whoever obeys me will not be put to shame,
    and those who work with me will not sin.'

All this is the book of the covenant of the Most High God,
    the law that Moses commanded us
    as an inheritance for the congregations of Jacob.
It overflows, like the Pishon, with wisdom,
    and like the Tigris at the time of the first fruits.
It runs over, like the Euphrates, with understanding,
    and like the Jordan at harvest time.
It pours forth instruction like the Nile,
    like the Gihon at the time of vintage.
The first man did not know Sophia fully,
    nor will the last one fathom her.
For her thoughts are more abundant than the sea,
    and her counsel deeper than the great abyss.

As for me, I was like a canal from a river,
    like a water channel into a garden.
I said, 'I will water my garden
    and drench my flower-beds.'
And lo, my canal became a river,
    and my river a sea.
I will again make instruction shine forth like the dawn,
    and I will make it clear from far away.

> I will again pour out teaching like prophecy,
>> and leave it to all future generations.
> Observe that I have not laboured for myself alone,
>> but for all who seek Sophia.
>
> *Ecclesiasticus 24:1-34*

The Wisdom of Solomon was written in the first century BC, and has strong Greek influence. In chapters 2–3, the contrasting ways of the wise and the foolish make the poor righteous man a target for the violence of his enemies, who condemn him to a shameful death. They despise his strange ways, the fruit of wisdom entering his soul whereby he knows and serves God, and calls him Father. The suffering righteous man and his kind are vindicated after their testing and conquer death, while the wicked are punished. These chapters act as the backdrop to the story of Jesus in all the Gospels, especially John.

Solomon goes on to praise Wisdom and pray for her blessing. The way he speaks of her attributes and the nature of his relationship with her informs John's account of Jesus throughout his Gospel:

> There is in her a spirit that is intelligent, holy,
>> unique, manifold, subtle,
>> mobile, clear, unpolluted,
>> distinct, invulnerable, loving the good, keen,
>> irresistible, beneficent, humane,
>> steadfast, sure, free from anxiety,
>> all-powerful, overseeing all,
>> and penetrating through all spirits
>> that are intelligent, pure, and altogether subtle.
> For Sophia is more mobile than any motion;
>> because of her pureness she pervades and penetrates all things.
> For she is a breath of the power of God,
>> and a pure emanation of the glory of the Almighty;
>> therefore nothing defiled gains entrance into her.
> For she is a reflection of eternal light,
>> a spotless mirror of the working of God,
>> and an image of his goodness.
> Although she is but one, she can do all things,
>> and while remaining in herself, she renews all things;
> in every generation she passes into holy souls
>> and makes them friends of God, and prophets;
>> for God loves nothing so much as the person who lives with Sophia.
> She is more beautiful than the sun,
>> and excels every constellation of the stars.
> Compared with the light she is found to be superior,
>> for it is succeeded by the night,
>> but against Sophia evil does not prevail.

> She reaches mightily from one end of the earth to the other,
>> and she orders all things well.
>>> *The Wisdom of Solomon 7:22–8:1*

In this next poem, Solomon speaks of Wisdom as a teacher whose heavenly authority informs wise and just rulers, with immortality – the victory of life over death – as one of her gifts. There are echoes in Jesus' exchanges with the Jewish and Roman authorities, and his promise of eternal life:

> I loved Sophia and sought her from my youth;
> I desired to take her for my bride,
>> and became enamoured of her beauty.
> She glorifies her noble birth by living with God,
>> and the Lord of all loves her.
> For she is an initiate in the knowledge of God,
>> and an associate in his works.
> If riches are a desirable possession in life,
>> what is richer than Sophia, the active cause of all things?
> And if understanding is effective,
>> who more than she is fashioner of what exists?
> And if anyone loves righteousness,
>> her labours are virtues;
> for she teaches self-control and prudence,
>> justice and courage;
>> nothing in life is more profitable for mortals than these.
> And if anyone longs for wide experience,
>> she knows the things of old, and infers the things to come;
>> she understands turns of speech and the solutions of riddles;
>> she has foreknowledge of signs and wonders
>> and of the outcome of seasons and times.

> Therefore I determined to take her to live with me,
>> knowing that she would give me good counsel
>> and encouragement in cares and grief.
> Because of her I shall have glory among the multitudes
>> and honour in the presence of the elders, though I am young.
> I shall be found keen in judgement,
>> and in the sight of rulers I shall be admired.
> When I am silent they will wait for me,
>> and when I speak they will give heed;
> if I speak at greater length,
>> they will put their hands on their mouths.
> Because of her I shall have immortality,
>> and leave an everlasting remembrance to those who come after me.
> I shall govern peoples,
>> and nations will be subject to me;

dread monarchs will be afraid of me when they hear of me;
    among the people I shall show myself capable, and courageous
    in war.
When I enter my house, I shall find rest with her;
    for companionship with her has no bitterness,
    and life with her has no pain, but gladness and joy.
When I considered these things inwardly,
    and pondered in my heart
    that in kinship with Sophia there is immortality,
    and in friendship with her, pure delight,
    and in the labours of her hands, unfailing wealth,
    and in the experience of her company, understanding,
    and renown in sharing her words,
I went about seeking how to get her for myself.

The Wisdom of Solomon 8:2-18

In this poem, heavenly secrets are the gift of heavenly Wisdom, just as in John's Gospel, only the heavenly Son of Man can speak of what he has seen:

With you is Sophia, she who knows your works
    and was present when you made the world;
she understands what is pleasing in your sight
    and what is right according to your commandments.
Send her forth from the holy heavens,
    and from the throne of your glory send her,
that she may labour at my side,
    and that I may learn what is pleasing to you.
For she knows and understands all things,
    and she will guide me wisely in my actions
    and guard me with her glory.
Then my works will be acceptable,
    and I shall judge your people justly,
    and shall be worthy of the throne of my father.
For who can learn the counsel of God?
    Or who can discern what the Lord wills?
For the reasoning of mortals is worthless,
    and our designs are likely to fail;
for a perishable body weighs down the soul,
    and this earthy tent burdens the thoughtful mind.
We can hardly guess at what is on earth,
    and what is at hand we find with labour;
    but who has traced out what is in the heavens?
Who has learned your counsel,
    unless you have given Sophia
    and sent your holy spirit from on high?

And thus the paths of those on earth were set right,
    and people were taught what pleases you,
    and were saved by Sophia.

The Wisdom of Solomon 9:9-18

Wisdom 10–19 celebrates Sophia's work in creation and the story of Israel, where she is the active agent of God who performs wonders and signs (Wisdom 10:16; 16:6). In these extracts, Sophia is responsible for feeding Moses and the people in the wilderness with water, quails and bread, guiding them by the pillars of cloud and fire, and consigning their enemies to darkness. What the Wisdom poetry says of Sophia, John says of Jesus:

Wisdom prospered their works by the hand of a holy prophet.
They journeyed through an uninhabited wilderness,
    and pitched their tents in untrodden places.
They withstood their enemies and fought off their foes.
When they were thirsty, they called upon you,
    and water was given them out of flinty rock,
    and from hard stone a remedy for their thirst.

The Wisdom of Solomon 11:1-4

Instead of this punishment you showed kindness to your people,
    and you prepared quails to eat,
    a delicacy to satisfy the desire of appetite;
For your sustenance manifested your sweetness towards your
    children;
    and the bread, ministering to the desire of the one who took it,
    was changed to suit everyone's liking.

The Wisdom of Solomon 16:2, 21

Therefore you provided a flaming pillar of fire
    as a guide for your people's unknown journey,
    and a harmless sun for their glorious wandering.
For their enemies deserved to be deprived of light
    and imprisoned in darkness,
    those who had kept your children imprisoned,
through whom the imperishable light of the law
    was to be given to the world.
The cloud was seen overshadowing the camp,
    and dry land emerging where water had stood before,
an unhindered way out of the Red Sea,
    and a grassy plain out of the raging waves,
where those protected by your hand passed through as one nation,
    after gazing on marvellous wonders.

The Wisdom of Solomon 18:3, 4; 19:7, 8

This final poem is from 1 Enoch, a collection of writings in five sections, dating from the third century BC to the second century AD. In 1 Enoch 42:1-3, not only does Sophia descend from heaven, she also ascends back to heaven because she finds nowhere on earth to live. The motif of Sophia's descent and ascent provides John with his basic image of the way divine grace engages with the world and brings salvation:

> Wisdom could not find a place in which she could dwell;
> but a place was found for her in the heavens.
> Then Wisdom went out to dwell with the children of the people,
> but she found no dwelling place.
> So Wisdom returned to her place
> and she settled permanently among the angels.[77]
>
> *I Enoch 42:1-3*

John's indebtedness to the poetry of the Jewish Wisdom tradition is widely acknowledged by present-day scholars. He does not quote any of it directly or adopt it uncritically. Unlike Ecclesiasticus 24, he sees Jesus rather than the law of Moses as the fullness of Sophia's revelation. He does not imagine Jesus-Sophia withdrawing from the world after his exaltation but realising his abiding presence in the coming of the Holy Spirit. And he uses the language of eternal life rather than immortality when he speaks of Jesus' victory over death. Nevertheless, John would count himself as one of Sophia's friends, albeit a critical one, and her poetry provides him with the basic theological grammar of his story of Jesus Christ, the Son of God.

---

77. Translated by James H. Charlesworth in his *The Old Testament Pseudepigrapha*, Volume 1, New Haven: Yale University Press, 1983, p. 33.

9. Jewish Wisdom trad.
10. Anti-Semitism?
15 SOPHIA.
18. 4 STYLES OF REL. TO GOD,
24. SON OF MAN
29 THE 7 SIGNS.
31 π of G - Eternal life.

50. Healing and Sin.
61. EATING + DRINKING. V. IMPORTANT.
69ff Times.
73 The Metaphor of Seeing.
74 JOHN HICK — Definition of faith

88. Quote.